The Secret of Contentment

The Secret of Contentment

WILLIAM B. BARCLEY

P U B L I S H I N G
P.O. BOX 817 • PHILLIPSBURG • NEW JERSEY 08865-0817

Printed in the United States of America

Library of Congress Cataloging-in-Publication Data

Barcley, William B.
  The secret of contentment / William B. Barcley.
    p. cm.
  Includes bibliographical references.
  ISBN 978-1-59638-191-9 (pbk.)
  1. Contentment–Religious aspects–Christianity. 2. Burroughs, Jeremiah, 1599-1646. Rare jewel of Christian contentment. 3. Contentment–Biblical teaching. 4. Bible. N.T. Philippians–Criticism, interpretation, etc.
I. Title.
  BV4647.C7B27 2010
  241'.4–dc22
                                    2010034069

To my children,
Leo, Anna, Luke, Maggie, Kate, and Will,
who are a constant source of joy and peace
in the midst of our hectic life together.

Contents

Preface

I DECIDED TO WRITE a book on contentment, not because I have contentment figured out and consider myself the most contented person in the world. Rather, I began to study and ultimately to write about contentment because I am often discontented. The lessons in this book are ones that I need to read and reread, continually applying them to myself. Pastors can sometimes slip into preaching aimed at the specific sins of others. Yet preaching is typically at its best when pastors preach to themselves as well as to their congregation. This book is definitely aimed at myself—as well as at all who share my struggle with contentment.

At the same time that I came to a stark realization of my own discontent, I also began to see how contentment is essential to holiness. Hebrews tells us that we are to pursue that holiness without which no one will see the Lord. Yet, without some level of contentment there cannot be true holiness. The discontented spirit does not rest in God's sovereign control. The discontented spirit desires more of the things of the world, an attitude that the Bible calls covetousness. Covetousness in turn leads to a host of other sins. So if we are going to achieve holiness, we must pursue contentment.

In this book I am mainly using the insights of others, especially the Puritan writers Jeremiah Burroughs (*The Rare Jewel of Christian Contentment*)[1] and Thomas Watson (*The Art of Divine Contentment*).[2] My goal by and large has been to take some of the wisdom of these "physicians of the soul" and, using modern language, apply it to a modern context. At the same time I have attempted to wed their insights to Paul's letter to the Philippians, Paul's letter of joy. I have gone beyond Burroughs and Watson in some places, but not very often.

I want to thank P&R Publishing for its willingness to work with me on this project and for its patience in seeing this come to fruition. This book was a long time in the making. I'm grateful to Allan Fisher, now of Crossway Books, for originally contacting me about writing for P&R and for his encouragement in the early stages of this work. Marvin Padgett skillfully guided me through an important process of re-writing which required me to think less like a scholar and more like a pastor. The book is much better as a result of this. Thanks too to Aaron Gottier, who led me through the final stages of editing.

I want to thank the two people who read almost all of what I write and give invaluable feedback—my friend and pastoral mentor Dr. Charles Wingard, Senior Pastor of Westminster Presbyterian Church, Huntsville, Alabama, and my wife, Kristy. I also want to thank the Session and dear congregation of Sovereign Grace Presbyterian Church in Charlotte for encouraging me to write and to have a ministry that extends beyond the church. I'm thankful for the study leaves they give me that allow me to take a break from my pastoral duties and focus on writing.

Finally, I want to thank my six children, Leo, Anna, Luke, Maggie, Kate, and Will. They are patient and understanding of my many hours out of the house doing ministry, and even allow me many undisturbed hours in the house working or writing in my study. Having a big, active family does not always lend itself to quiet reflection. There are many days that it seems we live in chaos, running from one event to the next or solving one crisis after another. Yet I wouldn't trade it for anything. My children give me great joy and peace in the midst of life's many storms. We as a family have made two major moves in the last ten years that have been very difficult on all of us. My kids have left friends and schools they loved to go to the unknown. But their ability to trust God (and Dad!) and adjust to their new surroundings—and even to prosper in the midst of change— has taught me much. Their sweet spirits and unconditional love have sweetened and softened me. In the midst of the mess and stress of everyday life, they have taught me much about contentment. This book is dedicated to them.

Introduction

✛

I BEGAN STUDYING contentment several years ago during a dark period in my life. I had just moved my family across the country to begin a new job. It was a great job—one that I had previously dreamed about and hoped for. But I had also applied for another position that would not require a move. I had my heart set on it. Yet I was not offered that job. This left me angry, bitter, discontent.

Now in a new state, in a new part of the country, I struggled with God's sovereignty. I found no delight in my new job. I found no delight in God and his plan for me. My anger and disappointment kept me up at night. I struggled to do the new work that I had been called to do. For a year I accomplished very little and performed poorly on the job.

My discontent also affected my family. I sulked around the house. I withdrew from my family. I was quick-tempered and yelled when something disrupted me. In my misery I'm afraid I made everyone else miserable. I became a self-absorbed, unloving husband and father.

It would be easy to look at the external symptoms—anger, moderate depression, lack of joy, being filled with self and unable to love—and see them as the main problem. But at the root of it all was the sin of discontent. I did not rest in God's sovereignty. I did not delight in him and his will. I sat on the throne of my life and wallowed in my own self-pitying resentment. I refused to yield to the One whose purposes and plans are perfect, who can use me as he sees fit, and who knows what is best for my life.

I know discontent. It is a great sin!

Evidently my own discontent places me in good company. Over one hundred years ago J. C. Ryle wrote, "Two things are said to be very rare sights in the world—one is a young man humble, and the other is an old man content. I fear this saying is only too true."[1] Almost four hundred years ago Puritan pastor Jeremiah Burroughs wrote of the "rare jewel" of Christian contentment. If it is true that contentment was rare in the days of Ryle and Burroughs, how much more is it true in our own day.

In his book *The Progress Paradox: How Life Gets Better While People Feel Worse*,[2] Gregg Easterbrook shows that while life in the Western world has dramatically improved over the last several decades, the level of happiness and contentment has declined. We live in an age of discontent.

Ours is a fast-paced world of tremendous change. We change jobs, change homes, even change the part of the country in which we live with tremendous frequency. Statistics and casual observation tell us that we also change spouses frequently. When we grow discontented in our current marriage, we move on to another. We are tempted to blame our culture for these things. But it is clear that the problem at the root is a sinful, discontented heart.

At the same time, our world does breed discontent in us. We are bombarded by advertisements that tell us we are incomplete or unfulfilled unless we have such and such a product. We have the Home Shopping Network, eBay, and glitzy, well-crafted commercials that attempt to lure our hearts after the things of this world. The modern, technological innovations are not bad in themselves. They can perhaps serve a good purpose (though personally I think Christians would be better off not watching the Home Shopping Network!). The problem is that they appeal to the sinful heart, which is already a discontented, idol-making factory (to use Calvin's expression).

This book addresses the heart of the matter—the discontent that lies within.

Not a lot of books have been written recently on the theme of Christian contentment. John Piper's *Desiring God*, though not explicitly addressing contentment, certainly speaks volumes on this subject. Piper's now famous line, "God is most glorified in us when we are most satisfied in him,"[3] is a biblical truth that we would do well to ponder.

The old Puritan writers, on the other hand, seem fond of speaking and writing of contentment. Indeed, the Puritans have produced two classics on the subject. The first is Jeremiah Burroughs's book *The Rare Jewel of Christian Contentment*. The second is Thomas Watson's *The Art of Divine Contentment*. The present work does not attempt to be original. I have blatantly, shamelessly ripped off ideas from these classic writings. Even the title, *The Secret of Contentment*, comes from what I would consider to be the heart of Burroughs's work. It is based on Paul's words in Philippians 4:11–12 that he has learned the "secret" or the "mystery" of being content. Contentment must be learned, and the way that we must pursue contentment is contrary to our natural ways of thinking. Burroughs speaks to the heart, calling us to a contentment that is the outcome of knowing God and delighting in his sovereign goodness and fatherly care. The present work simply seeks to meditate on and modernize Burroughs's important insights.

The idea for this book came from Kris Lundgaard's *The Enemy Within*. In that book, Lundgaard makes the writings of the Puritan John Owen accessible to modern readers. The insights that Lundgaard brings to light and applies are invaluable. He has done a great service to the church.

Burroughs and Watson are not as difficult to wade through as Owen. Everyone can and should read them. At the same time, I hope that this book can be helpful to those who are currently wrestling with their own discontent.

The rest of the story in our lives is that the move across country to the new job turned out to be one of the best moves of our lives. I loved the job, my colleagues, the place where we lived. It was a source of satisfaction and brought great joy. I am no longer at that job. God, in his providence, has moved us to a new work. But I learned and grew in ways that were invaluable for future ministry. Though disappointed and discontented initially, I can now look back and see God's hand at work. And I'm thankful for it.

I pray, however, that that earlier dark period in my life, which drove me to my knees and to the study of contentment, will bear fruit for the good of God's people, so that we might show forth his goodness to the world.

To God be the glory!

Discussion Questions

1. What are some situations in your life that have led you to question God's providence and resulted in a joyless discontent?

2. When are you the most contented in your life? What brings about the greatest discontent?

3. What are some ways that we can see God's hand at work, and take pleasure in it, while difficult circumstances are going on in our lives, rather than seeing later how God was working?

4. What aspects of modern life feed the sinful discontent of our heart? What steps can we take to avoid them?

5. Is a change in job or life situation always a sign of discontent? How can you tell the difference between a discontented desire for something new and a genuine submission to follow God's will for your life?

PART ONE

Pursuing Contentment

CHAPTER 1

The Nature of Christian Contentment

✤

NELSON ROCKEFELLER was once asked, "How much money does it take to make a person happy?" He reportedly answered, "Just a little bit more." This frank response gives us an insight into the human soul. We are tempted to think that we'd be happy with just a little bit more—though at times we are also tempted to admit that in reality happiness will require a LOT MORE!

Human beings always seem to want what they cannot have. This is true with jobs, houses, talents, and very often with spouses. The job we have never seems good enough, and the ideal job always seems just out of reach. Our houses are never big enough or never in just the right location; but we can't quite get the one we want. We recognize many of the talents that we have (and sometimes brag about them!), but we have a nagging envy of the other guy's abilities. Our divorce rate indicates that we are always looking for something more in marriage.

This problem is made worse by the fact that we think that if we had the right job, house, talent, or spouse, we'd be happy and content. But because these things are just out of reach, so is contentment—or so the common wisdom goes. The search for happiness based on our circumstances in life creates a restlessness and discontent in our souls.

Now listen to someone who did not think that life was about a constant search for something different or for more of what this life offers:

> I rejoiced in the Lord greatly that now at length you have revived your concern for me. You were indeed concerned for me, but you had no opportunity. Not that I am speaking of being in need, for I have learned in whatever situation I am to be content. I know how to be brought low, and I know how to abound. In any and every circumstance, I have learned the secret of facing plenty and hunger, abundance and need. I can do all things through him who strengthens me. (Phil. 4:10–13)

That's the apostle Paul. He testifies that he has learned to be content in any and every circumstance. His is not a constant search for the right circumstances that will bring him happiness. He is content wherever he is.

Paul's letter to the Philippians exudes Christian contentment. Not only does Philippians contain the classic passage on contentment quoted above, but contentment permeates the entire letter. Sixteen times in this letter Paul uses the noun *joy* or the verb *rejoice*. Joy refers to a state of gladness that typically occurs in Scripture with the recognition that God is in control no matter where we find ourselves. Joy is not a mere surface or momentary happiness. It goes deeper than that. The joyful heart is the contented heart, because it recognizes and delights in God's sovereign power and providential goodness.

Paul wrote Philippians from prison. He had been struggling with the question of whether his imprisonment would end in release or in death (1:19–26). He knows of others who are stirring up trouble for him while he is in chains (1:15–17). Yet, in spite of his circumstances, he has joy, and he exhorts the Philippians to rejoice. That's contentment!

If we want to learn contentment, a good place to start is by meditating on Philippians. Philippians will be the focus of much of this current study. We will learn from Philippians how to have contentment in afflictions and about the dangers of a murmuring, discontented spirit, among other things. But we will begin by looking at that classic biblical passage in which Paul describes for us the nature of Christian contentment, Philippians 4:11–13.

This passage teaches us several things about the nature of Christian contentment.

1. You can be content.

The first lesson we learn from Philippians 4:11–13 is that contentment is attainable. We know it is attainable because Paul has attained contentment. We might be tempted to think, "Well, Paul was an apostle; he was on a higher spiritual plane than I am. He may have attained contentment, but I can't."

But Paul did not attain contentment because he was a spiritual superstar. He says, "I can do all things through him who strengthens me." The same God who strengthens Paul also strengthens all who believe in Christ.

Philippians 4:13 is sometimes taken out of context and used in ways it was not intended to be used. Some take it to mean that there is nothing a Christian cannot do, because God is strengthening him or her. It almost becomes a motivational, self-help verse, in which people grit their teeth and say, "I can do this because God is strengthening me."

But it is important to recognize that when Paul says "all things," he doesn't mean that God gives you the ability to do whatever you want, even good things that you desire to do. Instead Paul is referring to God's empowering his people to acquire an important Christian virtue, namely, being content wherever God leads them. While growth in holiness does require effort and struggle on our part, ultimately we grow because of the power of God at work through his Holy Spirit within us.

The development of Christian contentment in a sinful, discontented heart is an impossible task. But what sinful human beings cannot achieve, God can and will. In addition, God promises to work in us, transforming us and conforming us into the image of Christ "from one degree of glory to another" (2 Cor. 3:18). God is carrying on his sanctifying work, so we can pursue contentment with confidence that God can develop this in our lives, just as he did in Paul's life.

The good news is that in the midst of your current struggles contentment can be yours. As you wrestle with a chronic health problem, a difficult job, or troubled relationships at home, you can have contentment as God gives you grace.

2. You need to learn contentment.

Twice in Philippians 4:11–13 Paul specifically says that he has "learned" to be content. In the Greek, Paul uses two different verbs to express the idea of learning. The first verb is a common word in the New Testament for learning something. The second verb, which appears in verse 12, is a little more unusual and occurs only here in the New Testament (though Greek writers outside the New Testament use it).

Paul's statement regarding learning in verse 12 is typically translated "I have learned the secret" (ESV, NASB, NIV, NLT, etc.). The verb is a verbal form of the Greek noun for "mystery." It was a verb that was used in the Greek mystery religions and sometimes took on the meaning "to be initiated" by various rites into these mystery religions.

Paul's use of this verb indicates that contentment does not come naturally. Not only must contentment be learned, but learning contentment is contrary to our normal (and sinful) ways of thinking. We cannot pursue Christian contentment the way the world pursues contentment, or even in the ways that we would be naturally inclined to pursue contentment.

This is what Jeremiah Burroughs refers to as "the mystery of contentment." The idea is not that Christianity attempts to be secretive, like the Greek mystery religions. The idea is, rather, that Christian contentment and how we pursue it are at odds with the thinking of this age and even of believers to the extent that the old sinful nature continues to influence our hearts and minds.

For example, the world says that to be content you need to get out of a bad situation. The Bible says that we are to find contentment in the midst of even the most difficult circumstances. The world says that contentment comes by getting what you want in this world. The Bible teaches that true contentment comes by being satisfied with God and longing for heaven. In this sense the truly contented Christian is always discontented in this life as he longs to be filled with God. We will discuss these matters in more depth in later chapters.

But the key idea here is that we have to work at contentment. We have to learn it. We have to study it. And we especially need to be "reprogrammed" in our thinking. God's way of achieving contentment, which is the only way to true contentment, is not our way.

I earlier referred to my own discontent when God closed one door and opened another, which required a major family move. Well, it recently happened again. In the process of God's moving us on to a new avenue of ministry, one door closed that would have kept us in the same general area, and another door opened that required a move to a new state. In fact, without going into detail, the circumstances were eerily similar to the earlier events. By his grace, however, God enabled me to delight in this work of his providence.

Don't get me wrong. My reaction was by no means perfect. Getting rejected for a job is never pleasant. As a friend who had also recently been turned down for a job wrote to me, "I wanted to say to them, 'You don't know what you're missing,' but then they also don't know how truly incompetent I can be!" There were some twinges of anger and a deep-seated pain that could be acute at times.

But there was also a joy and contentment that filled my heart most of the time. This came only by the grace of God, by repenting of my earlier sin of discontent, and by hours of study and reflection on contentment and God's sovereignty. Contentment is not the natural human response to difficulty. But we can—we must—learn it.

3. You will not be truly content until you learn to be content in every situation that you face in life.

Notice again Paul's description of his own contentment:

Not that I am speaking of being in need, for I have learned in whatever situation I am to be content. I know how to be brought low, and I know how to abound. In any and every circumstance, I have learned the secret of facing plenty and hunger, abundance and need. (Phil. 4:11–12)

He is content in every possible situation that he faces in life—in every circumstance, in great abundance, and in great need. In the same way, we have not truly learned contentment when we are content in some circumstances but not in others. Real Christian contentment entails being content in every situation in life.

Paul says, first, that he is content in plenty and in abundance. We may think that it is easy to be content when we are not in situations of hardship. But that's not true! Times of abundance and ease, though a great blessing, are often times when we become spiritually complacent. We easily forget God and pursue the things of the world, which in themselves never satisfy but only leave us longing for more.

We need to guard against an ungodly discontent when life is going well and God blesses us with material abundance and health.

But we also need to learn contentment in times of need. The contented Christian recognizes both the inevitability and the importance of afflictions. Paul knows hardship all too well. Remember, he is a prisoner as he writes this letter. Listen to what Paul writes to the Corinthians:

> As servants of God we commend ourselves in every way: by great endurance, in afflictions, hardships, calamities, beatings, imprisonments, riots, labors, sleepless nights, hunger. . . . We are treated as impostors, and yet are true; as unknown, and yet well known; as dying, and behold, we live; as punished, and yet not killed; as sorrowful, yet always rejoicing; as poor, yet making many rich; as having nothing, yet possessing everything. (2 Cor. 6:4–5, 8–10)

Can we truly say that when sorrowful, we still rejoice; that when poor, we are content to make many rich; that even when having nothing, we still possess all things?

Afflictions will come. This is true for all who live in a fallen world. But it is especially true for Christians who face the additional difficulties that come with being followers of Christ—persecution, self-denial, etc. Christ calls his people to suffer. As Burroughs writes, "Christ does not say, 'Recognize your crosses as crosses.' He says, 'Take up your cross daily.' "[1] Paul instructs Timothy, "Indeed, all who desire to live a godly life in Christ Jesus will be persecuted" (2 Tim. 3:12). Recognizing the inevitability of hardship helps us face them with a certain degree of contentment.

But hardship also has a God-ordained and Christ-exalting place in our lives. God uses affliction to sanctify us, to make us holy (cf. Rom. 5:3–5; Heb. 12:4–12). But afflictions work in this way only if we face them with a certain degree of contentment—accepting them as from the hand of God.

When a person has a bodily ailment—for instance, a stomach pain—and a doctor prescribes medicine to relieve the pain, if that person vomits the medicine up, not only will the medicine be ineffective with regard to the pain, it may also indicate a more serious medical problem. In the same way, when we cannot bear the hardships that God brings, it reveals a deeper problem in our souls. We're in spiritual danger.

We must recognize God's providence in every situation that we face, even when we are mistreated by sinful men. This was Joseph's perspective when he said to his brothers, who had sold him into slavery, "you meant evil against me, but God meant it for good" (Gen. 50:20). When we accept all hardships as from the hand of our heavenly Father, we grow in maturity, holiness, and contentment.

Furthermore, we must learn to be content with all types of afflictions, as well as with afflictions that last varying degrees of time. Sometimes Christians are able to endure one type of affliction but not another. Many Christians, for instance, will say that they are willing to suffer for the sake of Christ. But it becomes more difficult when we begin to talk about specifics, especially if they cut too close to our hearts' desires. Are we willing to endure if those hardships affect our families, our jobs, or our children? Often the loss of "the apple of one's eye," whether it be a spouse or a child, has led to anger, discontent, even a loss of faith.

With regard to types of afflictions, we also need to remember that afflictions often do not come one at a time. Rather, they come in bunches. Look at the sufferings of Job.

Hardships also last different lengths of time. Thankfully, many afflictions come and go quickly. Others last extended periods of time. Many Christians are forced to endure bodily ailments—headaches, backaches, etc.—for many years. Others, like hymn-writer William Cowper, suffer from depression that lasts much of their lives. The apostle Paul suffered from "a thorn in the flesh" that was especially troubling and plagued him for a long period of time. Three times he pleaded with God to take it away. Yet, though God could have done so, he chose not to. This thorn was sent to humble Paul and to reveal God's power at work in human weakness. It was purposeful. It resulted in glory to God.

How long are we willing to endure afflictions? Can we, like Paul, recognize them as coming from God, even though they are messengers of Satan (2 Cor. 12:7)? Are we, for the glory of God, willing to persevere through them, by the grace of God? We have no choice whether we face hardship. The choice is whether we glorify God in contentment or dishonor him in bitterness.

Contentment comes not by finding conditions suitable to us but by God's fashioning our spirits to our conditions.

4. You should understand contentment as "self-sufficiency."

This is tricky and could lead to misunderstanding, so we need to explore carefully the meaning of this.

The Greek word in verse 11 that is typically translated as "content" literally means "self-sufficient." In fact, the word was often used by Greek philosophers to describe what they held to be one of the chief virtues and was frequently described as non-attachment or not being dependent on others.[2] Now, it is important to recognize that this is decidedly *not* what Paul means by his use of the word here in Philippians. In fact, the type of "self-sufficiency" that Paul is describing here is different from worldly self-sufficiency in a number of ways.

First, this is not a "pull yourself up by your bootstraps" type of self-sufficiency. As we have already seen, it is attained only by the power of God. It is all of grace.

Second, it is not an individualistic self-sufficiency that says, "I don't need other people." The context of Philippians makes this clear. Paul recognizes the importance of the Philippians in his life and ministry. He is thankful for their "partnership in the gospel" (1:5), which has included both financial assistance (4:14–18) and the personal support of Epaphroditus (2:25–30). Paul also recognizes the need for their prayers, which will lead to his "deliverance" (or salvation, 1:19). The rest of Paul's letters bring out clearly his understanding that Christians need one another and can function properly as Christians only within the context of the community of believers.

Third, it is not a Stoic self-sufficiency. Stoicism was a popular philosophical system during Paul's day that essentially taught that everyone is subject to an impersonal power of fate that rules the universe. The key to life is not resisting but going along with what fate has determined. A famous illustration from Stoicism was that of a dog and a cart. Imagine a dog tied to the back of a cart. When the cart begins to move, the dog can choose either to go along and follow or he can choose to resist. Either way the dog will be pulled where the cart is going. The trip will be much more pleasant if he simply chooses to follow.

In light of this, Stoicism taught the importance of self-control and mastery of one's emotions. The person not in control of his thoughts and emotions will inevitably imitate the dog who resists the direction of the cart. To switch to a modern example, the Simon and Garfunkel song "I Am a Rock, I Am an Island" is in many ways a fitting description of this aspect of Stoicism. I will not let others affect me. "And a rock feels no pain; and an island never cries."

Although there might be aspects of Stoic teaching that have echoes in Paul, he would have stood firmly against this philosophical system. Paul's letters reveal a man who understood the importance of the bonds of Christian community, who loved and needed others. (See especially 2 Timothy as an example of this.)

What, then, does Paul mean by "self-sufficiency" in Philippians 4:11? In context, the idea of self-sufficiency here is that outward circumstances do not determine us. We are content no matter where God puts us, no matter what our situation. Furthermore, we do not rely on externals to bring us contentment. Instead it comes through the work of the Holy Spirit within us. God's grace at work within our hearts gives us an inner tranquility despite outward circumstances.

When little children are crying, we often give them things in an attempt to keep them quiet. If this works, it is the object that makes the child quiet and temporarily content. It is not the disposition of their spirits that has brought this about. Of course, the goal in parenting is to bring our children to the place where they are content apart from things, apart from always getting their way.

My brother-in-law tells the story of waiting in line at a bakery behind a young mother and her child. When they got to the counter, the little boy looked through the glass and said in a loud voice, "I want dat tookie." His mother responded calmly, "No, you can't have a cookie." The child repeated in a louder voice, "I want dat tookie. Gimme dat tookie." The mother repeated that he could not have a cookie. This went on for several minutes with the boy getting louder and louder and the mother clearly getting more and more exasperated. It was causing a scene in the bakery. Finally the mother gave up, bought the cookie, gave it to her child, and left the store.

All of us have faced the temptation, and most likely given in to it, of giving our children things simply to make them quiet. We also, however, recognize its dangers. Demanding children whose every need is catered to become a terror to parents—and to the rest of society. Furthermore, they never learn to have a quiet, contented spirit. This should be one of the goals of parenting.

But adults, too, need to learn this lesson. We need to develop the contentment, or "self-sufficiency," that is not based on externals but comes from within. This requires God's grace, but it also requires that we engage in the spiritual training of our hearts. Depending on our upbringing, this process might be more difficult for some than for others. Yet all of us have sinful hearts, and so all of us need the learning, training, and discipline required to achieve true Christian contentment.

There are times when it is right and legitimate to deal with a troubled soul by treating the symptoms with externals. When a person has lost all hope and becomes suicidal, that is not the time to talk about the need for extended training of the heart. We find other ways to keep that person from destroying himself. Other means, such as medication, vigorous exercise, or various diversions, can also be helpful at various times in life.

But we need to recognize that these external means only content us for a time. When various sets of circumstances present themselves again, discontent returns. Our world generally settles for quick fixes to heal the discontent of the soul. But true contentment only comes by addressing heart issues.

In light of all of this, we can now move toward a definition of Christian contentment. Burroughs defines it as follows: "Christian contentment is that sweet, inward, quiet, gracious frame of spirit, which freely submits to and delights in God's wise and fatherly disposal in every condition."[3]

It is hard to improve upon this clear, succinct, yet thorough definition. It brings together much of what we have seen so far.

First, contentment is inward. We can be calm on the outside, while inside trouble and disturbance rage. Contentment must be rooted in the heart.

Second, it is gracious. That is, it is rooted in God's grace, but it also graciously responds to every situation that one encounters.

Third, it delights in—or finds joy in—what God brings.

Fourth, it recognizes that every situation that we encounter in life comes from the hand of God. We must constantly be aware of God's providence and recognize that God has ordained all things for our good and for his glory.

Fifth, because our circumstances come from the hand of God, we must submit to them. The restless spirit, then, is the rebellious spirit.

Sixth, we must learn, like Paul, to be content in every condition. We have not learned contentment when we are ready to accept God's providence in some circumstances but not in others.

One final point: The type of contentment described in Philippians 4 reflects God's self-sufficiency. Theologians refer to self-sufficiency as one of God's attributes. God is not dependent on anyone. God does not need anyone or anything outside of himself. He is fully self-sufficient.

Now, we need to recognize that God is the Creator; we are creatures. We will never be self-sufficient in the way that God is. God has made us dependent beings—dependent on God first and foremost, dependent on others, dependent on other aspects of God's creation for survival.

Yet, to the extent that we achieve the "self-sufficiency" described in Philippians 4, we reflect in a small way this one aspect of the being of God. As our self-sufficiency reflects God's self-sufficiency, God's character is revealed in us. To put it differently, our contentment brings glory to God.

That is the goal of this book, and that should be the goal of our pursuit of Christian contentment—that God be glorified. In this sense, our study lines up wonderfully with John Piper's maxim, "God is most glorified when we are most satisfied in him."

May we achieve contentment, being satisfied in God, so that he might be glorified.

Discussion Questions

1. Most people harbor misperceptions about what will lead to contentment in their lives, whether they recognize them as misperceptions or not. What are some wrong ways of thinking that you have about how to attain contentment? What practical steps can you take to study and learn contentment and to correct those misperceptions in your life?

2. Have you learned, like Paul, to be content in any and every circumstance in life? What are some times that you struggle with contentment, and how can you begin to learn to be content in those times?

3. Do you find that you are more apt to be discontented in times of abundance or in times of need? Why?

4. How can the Bible's teaching on suffering and affliction help you to be content in the difficult times of life?

5. How is the "self-sufficiency" that Paul talks about in Philippians 4 different from the self-sufficiency of the world? In what ways do you find that you rely on externals to bring you happiness?

6. As you examine your heart, do you find that you have the quiet, sweet, gracious spirit that delights in all that God brings to you? How can you begin to develop the mindset that all that happens to us is from the hand of God?

CHAPTER 2

The Necessity of Christian Contentment

✥

IN THE MOVIE *Wall Street* the character Gordon Gekko famously declares, "Greed is good." Most people, however, are aware of the dangers of discontent and the benefits of contentment. Leo Tolstoy wrote a story called "How Much Land Does a Man Need?" It was about a successful peasant farmer who was not satisfied with what he had. He wanted more of everything.

One day he received an offer. For 1,000 rubles he could buy all the land he could walk around in a day. The only catch in the deal was that he had to be back at his starting point by sundown. Early the next morning he started out walking at a fast pace. By midday he was very tired, but he kept going, covering more and more ground. Well into the afternoon he realized that his greed had taken him far from the starting point. He quickened his pace, and as the sun began to sink low in the sky, he began to run, knowing that if he did not make it back by sundown the opportunity to become an even bigger landholder would be lost. As the sun began to sink below the horizon he came within sight of the finish line. Gasping for breath, his heart pounding, he called upon every bit of strength left in his body and staggered across the line just before the sun disappeared. He immediately collapsed, blood streaming from his mouth. In a few minutes he was dead. Afterwards his servants dug a grave. It was not much over six feet long and three feet wide—ironically answering the question posed by the title.[1]

Philosophers and writers throughout history have recognized the importance of contentment. Consider the following quotes:

Aesop: Be content with your lot; one cannot be first in everything.

Socrates: Contentment is natural wealth, luxury is artificial poverty.

Lin Yu-t'ang (Chinese philosopher and poet): The secret of contentment is knowing how to enjoy what you have, and to be able to lose all desire for things beyond your reach.

Benjamin Franklin: Contentment makes poor men rich; discontentment makes rich men poor.

Although many extol the virtues of contentment, the world's reasons for pursuing contentment are not necessarily biblical ones. So it is important for us to look at the biblical basis for contentment. Furthermore, since contentment requires learning, which itself necessitates effort and hard work, the weight of inertia can tempt us not to pursue it. If we begin the pursuit and experience growth pains, we'll be tempted to give up.

So we need to explore the question, why pursue contentment? Most of us are aware of the personal benefits that come from it. But the biblical reasons for contentment are more far-reaching than its personal benefits.

There are at least seven reasons why Christians need to pursue godly contentment.

1. God has commanded it.

The first reason to pursue contentment is that God has commanded it. Hebrews 13:5 tells us, "be content with what you have." We can add to this the numerous passages in Scripture where we are commanded to be joyful (e.g., Phil. 4:4). Joy, contentment's inseparable traveling companion, is the state of gladness that results from knowing that God is always in control. The joyful heart recognizes and delights in God's sovereignty.

The Bible, then, does not simply advise us that contentment and joy are good things. It commands us to be contented and joyful. Much of biblical religion boils down to this: trust and obey. As Christians, we are a people who seek to obey God. That is the way we glorify God. That is the way we enjoy him. Jesus said, "If you love me, you will keep my commandments" (John 14:15). If God has commanded us to be content, it is for our good and for his glory.

2. Contentment is a priceless treasure.

Second, we should pursue contentment because it is the greatest form of riches. Paul writes in 1 Timothy 6:6 that "there is great gain in godliness with contentment." In this context, Paul is contrasting the pursuit of worldly riches with the pursuit of contentment. In particular, he focuses our attention on what is really important. In terms of life and death it does not matter how much we have. We brought nothing into the world; we will take nothing out of it (1 Tim. 6:7). Eternity is what matters.

The key, then, is not the wealth of our outward state but of our inward state. Burroughs writes, "Contentment is the duty, glory and excellence of the Christian."[2] The apostle Peter exhorts wives to be adorned not with externals, like gold and fine clothing, but "with the imperishable beauty of a gentle and quiet spirit, which in God's sight is very precious" (1 Peter 3:3–4). External treasures can produce an earthly beauty, but that beauty is temporal and fleeting. The jewel of a contented heart, while sometimes evident in this life, is precious in God's sight and lasts into eternity.

My wife once received a string of pearls passed down through our family. I confess that I love those times when we dress up for a special night out and she wears a nice dress with her pearls. She is strikingly beautiful. But what makes my wife truly beautiful is her quiet, joyful, contented spirit.

An effective line of television advertisements proclaims, "Diamonds are forever." The commercials and slogan are appealing, even though we know deep down that the creators are guilty of false advertising. Material wealth cannot be compared to the radiant beauty of a quiet, peaceful, contented spirit.

Do you wish to be adorned with wealth and riches that surpass earthly riches and last for eternity? Then pursue contentment.

3. A murmuring spirit is great sin.

Third, a murmuring, discontented spirit is great sin. We will explore this in more detail in the next chapter. But Paul exhorts the Philippians, "Do all things without grumbling or questioning" (Phil. 2:14). The language that he uses brings to mind the grumbling of the Israelites in the wilderness. Numbers 11, in particular, gives us a glimpse of the nature of discontent, and God's response to it.

In looking at this passage, we need to begin by going back into Numbers 10. There we see two key incidents: the making of two silver trumpets (v. 2) and the people of Israel leaving Sinai (vv. 12ff.). The key themes throughout this chapter are that God is with his people and that God hears and is ready to help his people. Trumpet blasts "shall be a reminder of you before your God: I am the LORD your God" (v. 10). The point is not that God suddenly remembers them when they blow the trumpet. It is a sign and a reminder to the people of God's presence and his readiness to come to their aid (cf. v. 9).

Similarly, when God's people set out, "the cloud of the LORD was over them" (v. 34). Chapter 10 ends with these words:

And whenever the ark set out, Moses said, "Arise, O LORD, and let your enemies be scattered, and let those who hate you flee before you." And when it rested, he said, "Return, O LORD, to the ten thousand thousands of Israel." (vv. 35–36)

This is a beautiful picture of God's provision, protection, and presence with his people.

The beginning of Numbers 11 forms a stark contrast: "And the people complained in the hearing of the LORD about their misfortunes, and when the LORD heard it, his anger was kindled, and the fire of the LORD burned among them and consumed some outlying parts of the camp" (v. 1).

Numbers 11 presents a picture of what discontent involves and why it is so serious. First, grumbling entails forgetting God's presence and his blessings in our lives. The contrast between chapter 10, where God's presence is highlighted, and the beginning of chapter 11 points to this.

Second, discontent typically involves exaggerating the past. The initial incident of grumbling is followed almost immediately by another:

Now the rabble that was among them had a strong craving. And the people of Israel also wept again and said, "Oh that we had meat to eat! We remember the fish we ate in Egypt that cost nothing, the cucumbers, the melons, the leeks, the onions, and the garlic. But now our strength is dried up, and there is nothing at all but this manna to look at." (Num. 11:4–6)

The gist of this is, "Oh, remember how good things were in Egypt!" The reality, however, was that their suffering and burden were so bad that they cried out to God for deliverance. Remembering Egypt fondly was not only false, it was an offense to God who had graciously and miraculously delivered them. We also, in our discontent, sometimes paint a rosy picture of "the good old days"! This in turn leads to a failure to recognize that God has put us where we are right now and that he has put us there for a reason.

Third, grumbling is tied to our unbelief, questioning not only God's providence but also his provision. As we read on in Numbers 11, God in his grace provides meat—quail—for the people to eat. Furthermore, it does not come in meager portions. It comes in such an abundance that God says they will get sick of it. Yet Moses questions God's provision:

> But Moses said, "The people among whom I am number six hundred thousand on foot, and you have said, 'I will give them meat, that they may eat a whole month!' Shall flocks and herds be slaughtered for them, and be enough for them? Or shall all the fish of the sea be gathered together for them, and be enough for them?" And the LORD said to Moses, "Is the LORD's hand shortened? Now you shall see whether my word will come true for you or not." (vv. 21–23)

When we grumble, we don't believe that God is in control, and we question his ability to make good on his promises. At the root, then, is a lack of faith.

This chapter begins and ends with God's judgment, sending fire into their midst (v. 1) and a plague that struck down many (v. 33). Our discontent questions God's sovereignty, shows our failure to submit to his lordship, and is worthy of God's punishment. Grumbling is great sin.

4. Discontent is at the root of much of our sin.

Fourth, not only is discontent great sin, but it also is at the root of much sin in our lives. It too has many traveling companions. It clearly is at the root of covetousness. In its discussion of the tenth commandment, the Westminster Shorter Catechism (Q 80–81) says,

> Q. What is required in the tenth commandment?
> A. The tenth commandment requires full contentment with our own condition, with a right and charitable frame of spirit toward our neighbor, and all that is his.
>
> Q. What is forbidden in the tenth commandment?
> A. The tenth commandment forbids all discontentment with our own estate, envying or grieving at the good of our neighbor, and all inordinate motions and affections to anything that is his.

A coveting spirit is a discontented spirit because it desires what God has not given to us. A contented spirit, on the other hand, finds delight in what God has provided. It does not long for what it does not have. If we want to win the battle against a sinful, coveting spirit, then we must study contentment.

But inordinate desires, with their corresponding discontent, lead to a host of other sins as well. James tells us,

> But each person is tempted when he is lured and enticed by his own desire. Then desire when it has conceived gives

44

birth to sin, and sin when it is fully grown brings forth death. (James 1:14–15)

The word "desire" has the same Greek root as the verb "to covet" when the tenth commandment is quoted in the New Testament (cf. Rom. 7:7). Coveting, or sinful desire, takes shape in concrete acts.

James goes on to give an example of this in 4:1–2. Quarrels, fights, and even murder all stem from the passions and desires waging war within us. "You desire. . . . You covet," James says, and the sin of the heart is revealed in sinful words and deeds.

The Bible gives several accounts in which wrong desire leads to a host of other sins. David's desire for Bathsheba led to adultery and murder (2 Sam. 11). Ahab's desire for Naboth's vineyard led to bearing false witness against him and to murder (1 Kings 21). Eve's desire led to her and Adam eating from the forbidden tree and so plunging humanity into sin, death, and misery: "So when the woman saw that the tree was good for food, and that it was a delight to the eyes, and that the tree was to be desired to make one wise, she took of its fruit and ate, and she also gave some to her husband who was with her, and he ate" (Gen. 3:6).

It is vital, then, that we train the heart, learning to be content with what God has given us. When God comes and makes us new creatures in Christ, he gives us a desire for himself. We long for him as the deer pants for streams of water (Ps. 42:1). In sanctification, God takes our desires more and more away from the things of this world, placing them increasingly on himself. Contentment, then, is an integral part of our sanctification.

45

Martin Luther put it this way: "God does not dwell in Babylon, but in Salem"[3]—that is, not in confusion but in peace. God dwells in the soul that takes its rest in him.

5. A contented spirit shows our humble submission to God's will.

Fifth, a contented spirit demonstrates our submission to the sovereign control of God over our lives. A discontented spirit says, "I'm in control, and I will have what I want." A contented spirit accepts whatever God gives. It recognizes that God ordains all things and that he is sovereign over the events of our lives—whether in times of plenty and relative ease or in times of want and hardship.

During his Roman imprisonment, Paul was able to recognize—and rejoice in!—God's sovereign control of his situation. Far from hindering the progress of the gospel, his imprisonment had actually served to advance the gospel (Phil. 1:12). It had become known among the whole imperial guard (1:13), and other Christians were being emboldened by Paul's chains to preach Christ (1:14). Thus Paul rejoiced that the gospel was being preached, perhaps better than when Paul was free. He was in hardship, yet he recognized God's sovereign control. God was achieving his purposes.

6. Without contentment, we cannot experience the peace of God.

Sixth, without contentment we cannot experience the peace of God. It almost goes without saying that the contented spirit is the peaceful spirit, but we emphasize it nonetheless. Discontent breeds turmoil in the soul. Contentment leads to a peaceful, quiet spirit. Philippians, the same letter that commands us to rejoice and that presents Paul as the model of contentment, also speaks of the "peace of God, which surpasses all understanding" (4:7). The pursuit of contentment is in essence the pursuit of this peace.

7. The contented spirit is the worshipful spirit.

Seventh, by contentment we give to God the worship that is due him. Burroughs states that worship is not only "doing what pleases God," but also "being pleased with what God does."[4] Worship entails finding delight in God. But we find delight in God only when we are pleased with his sovereign control over our lives. When we are unsettled, restless, anxious, we cannot truly delight in God's presence.

In worship we say with the hymn-writer, "Whate'er my God ordains is right," and only in this way do we give to him the honor that is his due. In worship we exalt God as God and humble ourselves before him as his servants. We acknowledge his control, and we submit ourselves to his wiser determinations for our lives. True contentment, then, is at the heart of true worship.

If this last point is true, then there are great dangers in having a murmuring, discontented spirit. We will spend time considering this before moving on to our primary focus of how to pursue contentment.

Discussion Questions

1. Why is a discontented spirit so offensive to God?

2. What are some specific ways in your life that you have seen your own discontent lead to other sins?

3. Is the biblical truth that God ordains all things difficult to accept? Why or why not? How does embracing this truth help us have a contented spirit?

4. Think of people in your life who have the "jewel" of a contented spirit. How has this priceless treasure revealed itself in their lives?

CHAPTER 3

The Dangers of a Murmuring, Discontented Spirit

❖

ARE YOU CHARACTERIZED by a complaining, discontented spirit? Would others see you this way?

The story is told of a monk named Brother John. Brother John entered the "Monastery of Silence," and the abbot said, "Brother, this is a silent monastery; you are welcome here as long as you like, but you may not speak until I direct you to do so."

Brother John lived in the monastery for five years before the abbot said to him, "Brother John, you have been here five years now; you may speak two words." Brother John said, "Hard bed." "I'm sorry to hear that," the abbot said. "We will get you a better bed."

After another five years, Brother John was called by the abbot. "You may say another two words, Brother John." "Cold food," said Brother John, and the abbot assured him that the food would be better in the future.

On his fifteenth anniversary at the monastery, the abbot again called Brother John into his office. "Two words you may say today." "I quit," said Brother John. To this the abbot replied, "It is probably best; you've done nothing but complain since you got here."

This story, though humorous, hits home when we think about how often our words (and even worse our thoughts!) are marked by complaining and grumbling.

Contentment reveals the grace of God in our hearts. The negative side of this is also true—namely, murmuring and discontent reveal trouble in the soul. We often do not take our discontent seriously enough, blaming others when we feel that things are not going our way. But a discontented spirit points to a deeper spiritual problem. When discontent is present, we need to sit up and take notice.

Paul's letter to the Philippians not only teaches us about contentment, it also warns us about the dangers of discontent. Paul writes,

> Do all things without grumbling or questioning, that you may be blameless and innocent, children of God without blemish in the midst of a crooked and twisted generation, among whom you shine as lights in the world, holding fast to the word of life, so that in the day of Christ I may be proud that I did not run in vain or labor in vain. (Phil. 2:14–16)

The Greek word that Paul uses in verse 14, translated as "grumbling," is an example of what we call onomatopoeia, a word that sounds like what it describes. The word is *gon-*

gusmos, which, if you repeat over and over again, sounds like grumbling. The English word *murmur* functions in the same way.

More importantly, the word *gongusmos* was consistently used by the Greek translation of the Hebrew Old Testament (the Septuagint) to describe the grumbling of the Israelites in the wilderness. As we saw in chapter 2, and as we will see in more detail below, God treated this grumbling as great sin. Paul is essentially warning the Philippians not to be like the grumbling Israelites.

In considering what it means to do all things without grumbling or questioning, it is important to begin by pointing out what this does not mean. First, Paul does not advocate keeping all things inside and never sharing our struggles with friends. Paul shared his own deep struggles with friends, even while maintaining his commitment to do the will of God.

Second, Paul does not forbid a reverent complaint to God. We find faithful saints throughout Scripture who do this. The Psalms are filled with agonized pleading to God that he might rise up, reveal his glory, and rescue the psalmist from his plight. Of the first thirteen psalms, at least three (6, 10, and 13) might be considered "psalms of complaint," in which the psalmist reveals his struggle and wonders when God will act and come to his aid. We also find this throughout the prophets. Habakkuk 1:1–2:1 is a particularly striking example. Habakkuk complains to God about Israel's wickedness and complains again when God reveals his plan to chastise Israel by the hand of the more wicked Chaldeans!

When God's people pour out legitimate complaints, God is quick to answer and sometimes quick to deliver. The Israelites cried out in their affliction (Ex. 2:23–25). God heard and delivered them.

The point here is that there are legitimate forms of complaint and illegitimate ones. In the midst of our unrest, we need to examine two things: the frequency of our grumbling and the intensity of our grumbling. Do we grumble at every affliction or when any new wrinkle comes into our lives? Do we openly, trustingly make our complaint to God, or does our grumbling reflect disorder in our hearts? Ultimately it comes down to this: are we letting God be God, the Sovereign of the universe who orders all things for our good and his glory? Or do we consider God to be at our disposal, providing for us and ordering our lives as we think best?

We now turn our attention to Philippians 2:14–16 to explore what it teaches us about a murmuring, discontented heart.

1. Murmuring reveals corruption in the heart.

First, murmuring reveals corruption in the heart. Notice the important word "that" (which could also be translated "so that" or "in order that"), which connects verses 14 and 15: "Do all things without grumbling or questioning, *that* you may be blameless and innocent, children of God without blemish in the midst of a crooked and twisted generation." Being "blameless and innocent," as well as "without blemish," is dependent on doing all things without grumbling or questioning. To put it negatively, those who grumble in their spirits manifest corrupt and impure hearts.

This applies not only to our disposition in general but also to the manner of our obedience and service to God. We are called here to *do* all things without grumbling. It is possible, in other words, to obey God but to do it with a grumbling spirit. This is not true godliness. Even in our "obedience," a discontented spirit reveals a lack of holiness.

The way Paul ends this section in verse 16 confirms that a grumbling spirit reflects a spiritually dangerous situation. Verses 14–16 are all one sentence in the Greek, as they are in many of our English translations. They contain one key idea with several subordinate clauses. The main idea is the command that begins verse 14: "Do all things without grumbling or questioning." Everything else is dependent on that one command.

When Paul concludes this extended sentence, he says, "so that in the day of Christ I may be proud that I did not run in vain or labor in vain." Paul's running or laboring in vain seems to be in regard to the very salvation of the Philippians. The structure of the sentence, then, indicates that their grumbling is antithetical to the pursuit of that holiness without which no one will see the Lord (Heb. 12:14). The murmuring, discontented heart does not attain the Kingdom of God.

Does this mean that a contented spirit is a "work" we do to gain salvation? No. Paul's letters make clear that our salvation is all of grace (Eph. 2:8–9). But Paul is also careful to uphold human responsibility *and* divine sovereignty. We must, as Paul has just said in Philippians 2:12–13, "work out our own salvation with fear and trembling, for it is God who works within us to will and to work for his good pleasure." In addition, the absence of good works and of a transformed heart reveals the absence of God's grace.

Murmuring reveals the absence of grace in our hearts. We must see a grumbling, discontented spirit as the enemy of our souls.

The danger of grumbling is confirmed by looking at the larger biblical picture. Jude 15–16 says that the Lord will come

> to execute judgment on all and to convict all the ungodly of all their deeds of ungodliness that they have committed in such an ungodly way, and of all the harsh things that ungodly sinners have spoken against him. These are grumblers, malcontents, following their own sinful desires; they are loud-mouthed boasters, showing favoritism to gain advantage.

Three times in verse 15 various forms of the word "ungodly" are used. The nature of this ungodliness is spelled out in verse 16, where we see that the first two characteristics are those of being "grumblers" and "malcontents." In other words, Jude specifies that grumblers and malcontents are "ungodly sinners" upon whom God will bring judgment.

In the Old Testament it is also clear that God considers grumbling to be rebellion. Two consecutive incidents in Numbers 16 and 17 reveal this. In the aftermath of God's destruction of Korah, his family, and his followers, the Israelites "grumbled against Moses and against Aaron" (16:41). In response, God sends a plague, and 14,700 die. Immediately after this, in Numbers 17, God identifies his leaders through the budding of Aaron's staff. This incident is intended to put an end to the "grumblings" of the people (17:5, 10). The staff itself is to be publicly displayed as a sign "for the rebels" (17:10), so they will not die in judgment. Those who grumble against the Lord are guilty of rebellion against him. They are liable to God's judgment.

Three consecutive incidents from the book of Exodus also demonstrate that the complaining of God's people deserves God's judgment.

Immediately after God had delivered Israel from Egypt through the Red Sea (Ex. 14) and the Israelites had sung in celebration (Ex. 15:1–21), Moses leads the Israelites into the Desert of Shur where they travel for three days without finding water. Finally they come to Marah, where they cannot drink the water because it is bitter. At this point they "grumble" (15:24) against Moses, and God miraculously makes the water sweet. This chapter ends with a warning against the Israelites to keep the commands of God so that he does not bring on them the diseases that he brought on the Egyptians (15:26).

In Exodus 16, the Israelites travel to the Desert of Sin, where once again they grumble against Moses and Aaron, which in reality is grumbling against the Lord himself (16:8). This time they grumble because they do not have food. They even long for Egypt, where they had groaned under oppression but at least they had food to eat. In response, God reveals his glory and provides manna and quail for the Israelites to eat.

In Exodus 17, the people once again grumble because they have no water to drink. How does God respond to this? He provides water through Moses' striking the rock. But more significantly, God tells Moses that he will stand before Moses "on the rock" (17:6). By standing on the rock, God identifies himself with it. When the rock is struck, God is struck. God takes the blow for his people. He bears their punishment. This foreshadows the death of Christ, the perfect God-man who bore the punishment for his people. So the apostle Paul tells us that the rock in the wilderness was Christ (1 Cor. 10:4).

The point here is that the grumbling and discontent of the Israelites is so serious that God must provide atonement. But he graciously does so by bearing the punishment for his people. God was struck for the grumbling of his people, which is a great sin.

In all three incidents the Israelites are confronted by a serious situation. The lack of food and water took them to the brink of their lives. Water is especially critical in the desert, where you cannot survive long without it. All three incidents portray a situation of desperation and urgency. We can perhaps be sympathetic to the Israelites' plight. We may be tempted to give them some slack in their grumbling. Life seems to be ebbing away.

But while God knows their needs and is ready to meet them, he cannot ignore their murmuring. He views it as great sin and as rebellion against his sovereign rule over them. Their sin deserves his wrath and judgment.

I have taken spiritual inventory of the times that I have had a grumbling, complaining spirit this week. It is not a pretty picture. Let me give just a few examples.

I grumbled in my spirit when I had to sit in traffic (a common occurrence in Charlotte!) and arrived at the office ten minutes later than I had planned. I grumbled to my wife when she did not buy the nutrition bars that I normally eat as a snack during the day. I grumbled when I found out, a few hours ahead of time, that I had been put on a volunteer list to help with a particular task at my daughter's middle school basketball game. I grumbled when I realized the half-and-half that I put in my coffee at work had gone bad. I grumbled when I arrived at church one evening for a meeting and found some workers stripping and waxing the floors, forcing us to move our meeting to a different location. I grumbled when my kids were making too much noise in the hall outside my home study, disturbing my time of sermon preparation. And that's just the beginning!

All of this is petty compared to the extreme situation of hardship faced by the Israelites in the wilderness. They have been taken from what was familiar to them and are in a dangerous and hostile place. They have no home, no bed, no creature comforts. And now they have no food or water. Yet God views their grumbling as rebellion against him.

We face various forms of affliction in our lives. Some amount to minor inconveniences, while others are severe hardships. Especially in these latter situations, we are tempted to think ourselves justified for a grumbling, discontented spirit. But God does not.

Ultimately our afflictions, our external circumstances, do not cause our discontent. They are simply occasions for the corruption of our heart to reveal itself. The deeper problem is a heart problem. Rebellion lies deep in the human heart. And this rebellion deserves God's punishment.

But Exodus 17 reveals the grace of God toward his people. Not only is God the holy God who must punish sin, he is also the gracious God who takes the punishment for his people's sin. He deals with us not as our sins deserve but mercifully, as his beloved children.

2. Murmuring is beneath the dignity of the children of God.

This leads us to the second lesson that we learn from Philippians 2:14–16—namely, that murmuring is beneath the dignity of the children of God. In verse 15 Paul specifically reminds them that they are "children of God"—"that you may be blameless and innocent, children of God without blemish in the midst of a crooked and twisted generation." All of the riches of God's mercy and blessing are available to us. This should give to God's children a composure that does not mark unbelievers. As Burroughs has said, our grumbling is like the child of a king crying and stomping his feet when he loses a toy.

When we are tempted to complain in our hearts against God, we need to stop and consider what God has done for us. First, God has purchased us for himself. Paul writes in 1 Corinthians 6:19–20, "You are not your own, for you were bought with a price. So glorify God in your body." That price was the death of the Lord Jesus Christ. He endured the agony of the cross, but more importantly he bore the wrath of God that we deserved for our sins. The price of our redemption was great. The affliction of Christ makes all of our afflictions small by comparison. Instead of grumbling, our lives should be filled with thanksgiving.

Second, God has made us to see our sin. This is a great blessing because we cannot turn to the Savior unless we see the weight of our sin. Furthermore, it is the burden of our sin that causes us to love the Savior. Christ said, "he who is forgiven little, loves little" (Luke 7:47). But finally, the burden of our sin should swallow up all other burdens in our life. The momentary afflictions of this life are nothing compared to the great weight of sin that merits the eternal wrath of God. When hardships come our way, we need to look inward at the sin that continues to plague our hearts, and we need to look outward at the Savior who has taken the guilt of our sin on himself.

Third, God has turned us away from ourselves. Our self-love and our pursuit of self-interest hinder us from turning to God in faith and repentance. In making us new creatures in Christ, God breaks the power of self. In conversion, we surrender everything to him.

But murmuring means that we are holding back from full surrender. In grumbling we assert self, failing to submit to God's rule over us. We need to pray that God would make that initial regenerating work of turning us from ourselves a daily reality in our lives.

Fourth, God has put all things at our disposal. Paul makes this clear several times in his letters. Consider the following passages:

> For all things are yours, whether Paul or Apollos or Cephas or the world or life or death or the present or the future—all are yours, and you are Christ's, and Christ is God's. (1 Cor. 3:21–23)

> What then shall we say to these things? If God is for us, who can be against us? He who did not spare his own Son but gave him up for us all, how will he not also with him graciously give us all things? (Rom. 8:31–32)

> We put no obstacle in anyone's way, so that no fault may be found with our ministry, but as servants of God we

commend ourselves in every way: by great endurance, in afflictions, hardships, calamities, beatings, imprisonments, riots, labors, sleepless nights, hunger; by purity, knowledge, patience, kindness, the Holy Spirit, genuine love; by truthful speech, and the power of God; with the weapons of righteousness for the right hand and for the left; through honor and dishonor, through slander and praise. We are treated as impostors, and yet are true; as unknown, and yet well known; as dying, and behold, we live; as punished, and yet not killed; as sorrowful, yet always rejoicing; as poor, yet making many rich; as having nothing, yet possessing everything. (2 Cor. 6:3–10)

Each of these passages teaches that God has given us everything. This should be our attitude even, as in the last passage, in the midst of affliction.

We often take too narrow a view of life in this world. We need a broader vision of all that God has done and is doing for us. John Newton writes,

Suppose a man was going to York to take possession of a large estate, and his chaise [carriage] should break down a mile before he got to the city, which obliged him to walk the rest of the way. What a fool we should think him, if we saw him wringing his hands, and blubbering out all the remaining mile, "My chaise is broken! My chaise is broken!"[1]

Why should we grumble and complain at the momentary troubles and afflictions of this life when God has given all things to us? The concerns of this world are nothing compared to the inheritance laid up for God's saints.

3. Murmuring affects our witness for Christ.

Finally, Philippians 2:14–16 teaches us that murmuring affects our witness for Christ. Paul's teaching on the Christian life consistently has an outward, evangelistic focus. This is true in Paul's teaching on contentment as well. We should not think of contentment solely in an individualistic way, in terms of the peace that it brings to us. We need to think of it evangelistically. The contentment of believers reveals to the world the glory of God. The glory of God shines forth through the contented Christian—precisely Paul's point in Philippians 2:15!

Paul says that, as children of God, believers "shine as lights in the world . . . in the midst of a crooked and twisted generation." But in context this seems dependent on their doing all things "without grumbling or questioning." A murmuring spirit dims the light, preventing discontented Christians from shining like stars.

The evangelistic thrust of this passage may also be present in the first part of verse 16. Many translations read "holding fast to the word of life," but the phrase could also be translated "holding forth the word of life." The implication again would be that the evangelistic work of the church, presenting the gospel to the world, is marred by the murmuring and discontent of its members.

Why does grumbling diminish the church's witness? There are at least two reasons for this. One, a discontented spirit proclaims self and not Christ (see 2 Cor. 4:5—we can proclaim self or proclaim Christ, but not both). The grumbling, discontented person is a self-absorbed person. A witness must point others away from himself and to the Savior.

Two, grumbling makes us like the world, not set apart from it. Unbelievers by their very nature are discontented. Augustine said the heart is restless until it finds its rest in God. The world is not looking for more of the same. The heart of the unbeliever has a longing that this world cannot satisfy. In the midst of this unrest and confusion, the church must offer an alternative—hearts that are at rest and at peace, secure and content in their God.

We must pursue contentment, not only for the good of our own souls, but also for the sake of those who are lost and thirsty because they do not know the God of peace.

How, then, do we attain godly contentment? We turn our attention now specifically to the pursuit of contentment, recognizing that attaining a godly virtue requires godly, and not worldly, means.

Discussion Questions

1. Would you say that you are frequently marked by a grumbling, complaining spirit? Examine the nature of the complaints in your life. Are they reverent complaints, like we find in Scripture, or are they discontented, sinful complaints? How can you tell the difference?

2. Are you tempted to think that times of complaining are caused by outward circumstances, instead of revealing corruption in your heart? What are some ways that you can begin to train your mind to think differently about this?

3. Can you think of specific times when your grumbling or complaining has hindered your witness for Christ? Think

creatively about those situations and how you could have turned them into opportunities for evangelism.

4. How is our grumbling an indication of holding back from giving our whole selves to Christ? Take time to pray for God's grace and that you would completely surrender to him.

PART TWO

The Mystery of
Contentment

CHAPTER 4

The Contentment of the Discontented Christian

✠

A FRIEND ONCE SAID to me, "In Philippians 4 Paul sounds so contented. But one chapter earlier, in Philippians 3, he sounds discontented. How can this be?"

Indeed, the contrast is striking. In Philippians 4:11–13 Paul says that he has learned the secret of being content in any and every situation. But listen to him just one chapter earlier, in Philippians 3:12–14:

> Not that I have already obtained this or am already perfect, but I press on to make it my own, because Christ Jesus has made me his own. Brothers, I do not consider that I have made it my own. But one thing I do: forgetting what lies behind and straining forward to what lies ahead, I press on toward the goal for the prize of the upward call of God in Christ Jesus.

This passage sounds like the antithesis of what we see in chapter 4. Here Paul is decidedly discontented. He has not attained; he presses on; he strains forward. Isn't this the opposite of contentment?

It is unlikely that Paul has contradicted himself in the space of a few paragraphs in the same letter. The discontented pursuit that Paul describes in Philippians 3, then, must be directly related to the contentment of chapter 4. In other words, a godly discontent is present in the contented Christian.

This godly discontent is part of the mystery of contentment. The fact that discontent would be the path to godly contentment sounds strange to our ears. But as we saw in our study of Philippians 4:11–13, contentment does not come naturally. How we pursue biblical contentment is contrary to our human ways of thinking. Contentment is a mystery. We need to retrain our minds to achieve it.

Let's look more closely at Paul's description of his own restless pressing on in Philippians 3:12–14, applying it to the pursuit of Christian contentment.

1. The contented Christian is the dissatisfied Christian.

First, this passage teaches us that we are most content when we are not satisfied with our accomplishments. Paul is an old man. He is nearing the end of his life. He has been a Christian for many years. And yet he has not attained what he desires but presses on to take hold of it.

When we read in verse 12 that Paul has not already obtained "this," we are forced to look back into the previous section to see what "this" refers to. It is clear that "this" refers to his knowledge of Christ. He states his desire "that I may know him and the power of his resurrection, and may share his sufferings, becoming like him in his death" (3:10). He presses on that he might know Jesus Christ and become like him in his

68

sufferings and death, ultimately to attain "the resurrection from the dead" (3:11).

The contented Christian is the most contented person in the world; yet he is also the most unsatisfied. He longs to know Christ, to have more intimate knowledge of him, to be conformed to his image, to share in his work. This side of glory, the Christian will never attain what he desires. He will always want more.

Burroughs puts it this way, "A soul that is capable of God can be filled with nothing else but God."[1] When God comes and transforms the heart of a sinner, so that he can by faith know God, God gives to him a desire and a longing after himself. The things of this world do not satisfy him. The most glorious riches, the deepest relationships, and the most peaceful landscapes in the world pale in comparison to true communion with the living God. And this communion is what the Christian seeks. He pursues until his thirst is quenched.

The psalmist writes,

As a deer pants for flowing streams,
     so pants my soul for you, O God.
My soul thirsts for God,
     for the living God.
When shall I come and appear before God? (Ps. 42:1–2)

In another psalm, the psalmist declares,

Whom have I in heaven but you?
     And there is nothing on earth that I desire besides you.
My flesh and my heart may fail,
     but God is the strength of my heart and my portion
          forever. (Ps. 73:25–26)

These are the cries of the contented Christian who knows his God but who longs to know him more.

In this life we can experience the sweetness of communion with God. But we cannot know him fully. We cannot know him as we will someday. I believe it was Augustine who said, "I have seen the depths, but I cannot find the bottom." And so the contented Christian presses on to know God more fully, longing for the day when he will see him face-to-face.

Thomas Kelly's hymn describes this well:

Keep us, Lord, O keep us cleaving
To thyself and still believing,
Till the hour of our receiving
Promised joys with thee.

Then we shall be where we would be,
Then we shall be what we should be;
Things that are not now, nor could be,
Soon shall be our own.[2]

2. The contented Christian is the single-minded Christian.

Second, Philippians 3:12–14 teaches us that we must be single-minded in this pursuit. Paul says in verse 13, "one thing I do." One thing. Other places in the Bible also make mention of "one thing." David says, "One thing have I asked of the LORD, that will I seek after: that I may dwell in the house of the LORD all the days of my life, to gaze upon the beauty of the LORD and to inquire in his temple" (Ps. 27:4). This desire is similar to Paul's in Philippians 3. Both want to know the Lord better.

In Luke 10 we find the account of Jesus at the home of Mary and Martha. Martha is busy with all of the preparations, while Mary sits at Jesus' feet listening to him as he teaches. Martha gets irritated and complains to Jesus, asking him to tell Mary to help her. Jesus responds, "Martha, Martha, you are anxious and troubled about many things, but one thing is necessary. Mary has chosen the good portion, which will not be taken away from her" (vv. 41–42). "One thing" is necessary—to commune with Christ and learn from him.

Martha does a very good thing. She serves the Lord. But she is distracted in all of her preparations. We too, especially when serving Christ energetically, can lose track of what is important. We get distracted, and we lose sight of the "one thing." How often we choose the good over the best!

We have looked at three "one thing" passages, but we need to look at each one in its context. In Psalm 27 we have the pursuit of "one thing" in the context of worship—dwelling in the house of the Lord, gazing upon his beauty, inquiring in his temple. In Luke 10 Mary is sitting and learning from Jesus. But in Philippians 3 the context is Paul's ministry. In other words, while the first two instances are perhaps examples of what we might call quietism, the third example is clearly the pursuit of the "one thing" in the context of activism.

The goal, in other words, is the same—to know the Lord, to be conformed to his image, ultimately to attain the resurrection from the dead when believers are fully conformed to the image of Christ. But God has given us various ways to pursue that goal. There's a time for worship, a time for learning, and a time for active ministry. Yet, even though the tasks change, the "one thing" remains—knowing Christ more deeply and being conformed to his image.

As the apostle to the Gentiles, Paul's primary task was an evangelistic one—preaching the gospel, making disciples, establishing churches. In other words, he sought to make Christ known. Today many churches have a vision statement along these lines: "Knowing Christ, making him known." This is a fine statement and goal. Yet in this passage we can summarize Paul's goal as "knowing Christ *by* making him known."

In Philippians 3:10, knowing Christ includes knowing both the power of his resurrection and the fellowship of his sufferings, becoming like Christ in his death. This means that the knowledge of Christ will require pain and hardship in the life of the Christian. This leads to our third point about Philippians 3:12–14.

3. The contented Christian strains forward in pursuit of a heavenly goal.

Third, the contented Christian's restless pursuit to know Christ involves straining forward to attain his heavenly goal. Listen again to Paul's words in Philippians 3:13–14: "But one thing I do: forgetting what lies behind and straining forward to what lies ahead, I press on toward the goal for the prize of the upward call of God in Christ Jesus." The language that Paul uses of "straining forward" carries with it the notion of pain, struggle, effort, discipline. One Greek dictionary translates the Greek word used here as "to exert oneself to the uttermost, stretch out."

One image that captures the sense is that of a runner sprinting for the finish line. His strength is spent, but he gives it his all. Then as he approaches the finish line he stretches forward to be the first to cross the line. Our family has been to many track meets and cross-country events (our son runs in them). We have seen many a runner come to the end and simply collapse because of the effort he has made.

This is what Paul says about the nature of the Christian life. It is not easy. It requires hard work, discipline, and great effort. It means pressing on when we don't think we can go any farther. And it is going to mean great pain—pain from the sacrifice that it requires, pain from the scoffing and persecution of the world.

In the 1992 Summer Olympics, a British runner named Derrick Redmond was the favorite to win the 400 meter race. He was a great runner, and he started off running well. But as he was going down the backstretch Redmond suddenly fell to the ground. He had ripped his hamstring muscle. For several moments he lay on the ground in great pain, holding his leg, while the rest of the runners ran around the track to finish the race.

Then suddenly he got to his feet and began, as best he could, to make his way around the track. He alternated between hopping on his good leg and hobbling in great pain on both legs. It was obvious that his intention was to finish the race.

The crowd began to recognize what was taking place, and they rose to their feet to cheer him on. As he came around the fourth and final turn, the entire crowd was standing and cheering. Suddenly Derrick Redmond's father came onto the track, and briefly father and son embraced.

Then the two of them, father supporting son, walked to the finish line.

Derrick Redmond did not win the race that day. But he came to run and to finish, and he pressed on to do that, in spite of the pain and agony that it caused him. He was a champion runner. He had won many races in the past. But he was intent on finishing this one.

In the same way, Paul says that he presses on toward the goal. Derrick Redmond was pressing on toward an earthly goal. The Christian presses on toward a heavenly one: "I press on toward the goal for the prize of the upward call of God in Christ Jesus." Later in Philippians 3, Paul tells the Philippians that "our citizenship is in heaven" (v. 20). We will return to this theme later by looking at the contentment of longing for heaven. But it is important for the Christian who presses on to remember that while we do the work of Christ on earth, ultimately this world is not our home. Our eyes must be fixed on heaven.

One final point about Philippians 3:12–14: The Christian presses on and strains forward in the knowledge of and because of the fact that Christ Jesus has taken hold of him (3:12). For Paul, God's grace always takes preeminence. We work because God has worked to make us his and is working within us.

Just one chapter earlier Paul says, "work out your own salvation with fear and trembling, for it is God who works in you, both to will and to work for his good pleasure" (2:12–13). The striving of the Christian is not futile, a restless grasping after the wind. It is done knowing that Christ has already completed the necessary work for our salvation. He has made us his own, and we belong to him. And Christ, through his Spirit, continues to work through us as we complete the work that God has given us to do.

That should quiet our hearts and give peace to our troubled souls. Still, the peaceful, contented Christian, who knows that his eternity is secure in Christ, presses on to know Christ better. Content, yet discontent. This is a mystery. But it is the way to true peace.

Raymond Lull, missionary to the Muslims in North Africa, was one who pressed on to know Christ and to share his sufferings. He was teaching Arabic in Europe at the age of seventy-nine when he was compelled to return to North Africa. His biographer, Samuel Zwemer, describes it this way:

> His pupils and friends naturally desired that he should end his days in the peaceful pursuit of learning and the comfort of companionship.
>
> Such however was not Lull's wish. His ambition was to die as a missionary and not as a teacher of philosophy. . . . Lull's own motto [was], "He that lives by the life can not die." . . . In Lull's contemplations we read . . . "Men are wont to die, O Lord, from old age, the failure of natural warmth and excess of cold; but thus, if it be Thy will, Thy servant would not wish to die; he would prefer to die in the glow of love, even as Thou wast willing to die for him."
>
> The dangers and difficulties that made Lull shrink back . . . in 1291 only urged him forward to North Africa once more in 1314. His love had not grown cold, but burned the brighter. . . . He longed not only for the martyr's crown, but also once more to see his little band of believers [in Africa]. Animated by these sentiments he crossed over to Bugia on August 14,

and for nearly a whole year labored secretly among a little circle of converts, whom on his previous visits he had won over to the Christian faith. . . .

At length, weary of seclusion, and longing for martyrdom, he came forth into the open market and presented himself to the people as the same man whom they had once expelled from their town. It was Elijah showing himself to a mob of Ahabs! Lull stood before them and threatened them with divine wrath if they still persisted in their errors. He pleaded with love, but spoke plainly the whole truth. The consequences can be easily anticipated. Filled with fanatic fury at his boldness, and unable to reply to his arguments, the populace seized him, and dragged him out of the town; there by the command, or at least the connivance, of the king, he was stoned on the 30th of June 1315.[3]

Raymond Lull died as a martyr at the age of eighty. Advanced in years, like the apostle Paul, Lull did not rest in the work already done. He pressed on toward the goal for the prize of the upward call of God in Christ Jesus. His love for Christ and his security in Christ (knowing that he could not die) compelled him to know Christ *by* making him known— even unto death. This is godly discontent.

Daniel tells us, "the people who know their God shall stand firm and take action" (Dan. 11:32). The contented Christ knows his God *and* longs to know him better in sacrificial service.

Discussion Questions

1. The idea that the contented Christian is also decidedly discontented sounds like a contradiction. Have you

experienced times in your Christian walk when you have known peace and contentment, while longing to know Christ more? In an attempt to get your mind around this biblical truth, stop and think of how you might explain this to someone else.

2. Have you experienced being distracted from the "one thing" of knowing Christ, even perhaps in the midst of serving him? How can you be single-minded throughout all of the various activities that God has called you to perform?

3. What are some things that make the Christian life so difficult and, at times, so painful? How can you encourage others and be encouraged by others in this struggle?

4. Do you have the sense of God calling you to serve him in some way as you seek to know him by making him known?

CHAPTER 5

Finding Contentment in the Midst of Affliction

✥

AFFLICTION is the greatest test of our contentment. When our world is falling apart, trust in God's sovereignty wavers, and a peaceful frame of mind becomes unsettled. Our faith is challenged. We learn then the depth of our contentment.

When sickness comes, when tests reveal the spot to be cancer, when we lose our job, when a child is taken away from us, when our good name is unjustly defamed, how do we respond?

Paul has learned the secret of being content in any and every situation in life. Philippians demonstrates this, as Paul writes this joyful letter from prison. What sustains Paul during his hardships and trials? How can he find contentment in the midst of the most difficult circumstances?

At the root of Paul's contented response to suffering is his recognition that affliction is inevitable. Christ made this clear to Paul at his conversion. In Acts 9, after Christ appeared to Paul on the Damascus road, he instructed Ananias to go to Paul and lay his hands on him. Ananias balked, fearing for his own safety. But Christ responded, "Go, for he is a chosen instrument of mine to carry my name before the Gentiles and kings and the children of Israel. For I will show him how much he must suffer for the sake of my name" (Acts 9:15–16).

Paul's conversion was a call to ministry. It was also a call to suffer. Suffering permeates Paul's preaching and his letters—not only his own suffering, but also the inevitability of suffering for all Christians.

Paul instructed the recently formed churches in Lystra, Iconium, and Antioch that "through many tribulations we must enter the kingdom of God" (Acts 14:22). He told Timothy that "all who desire to live a godly life in Christ Jesus will be persecuted" (2 Tim. 3:12). It is simply inevitable. But more than that, it is a gift. Paul writes to the Philippians, "For it has been granted to you that for the sake of Christ you should not only believe in him but also suffer for his sake" (Phil. 1:29). Both believing and suffering are "granted"; that is, they are gifts from God.

Earlier we discovered that Paul desired to know Christ and the power of his resurrection, but also to share in Christ's sufferings (Phil. 3:10–11). Part of the believer's union with Christ, a prominent theme in Paul's letters, is that he takes part in the suffering of Christ. Paul learned this well on the Damascus road, when Christ said to him, "Saul, Saul, why are you persecuting me?" Because Christians are united to Christ, when they suffer, Christ suffers.

Jesus himself teaches that the suffering of Christians is directly related to his own suffering. He tells his disciples that the world will hate them because it hates him (John 15:18–19).

He goes on to say, "If they persecuted me [and they did!], they will also persecute you" (15:20). And once more he instructs them, "In the world you will have tribulation. But take heart; I have overcome the world" (John 16:33).

We must recognize the inevitability of suffering and hardship. On the one hand, all suffer. Sickness, failed relationships, death of loved ones, failures, and setbacks are inescapable. They are simply part of life in a fallen world. But Christians especially will face persecution of different kinds. Accepting the reality of suffering is a large part of the battle to find contentment in the midst of our afflictions.

We can also learn much by studying Paul's own reactions to his afflictions. In Philippians 1 Paul offers reflections on his current imprisonment:

> I want you to know, brothers, that what has happened to me has really served to advance the gospel, so that it has become known throughout the whole imperial guard and to all the rest that my imprisonment is for Christ. And most of the brothers, having become confident in the Lord by my imprisonment, are much more bold to speak the word without fear. Some indeed preach Christ from envy and rivalry, but others from good will. The latter do it out of love, knowing that I am put here for the defense of the gospel. The former proclaim Christ out of rivalry, not sincerely but thinking to afflict me in my imprisonment. What then? Only that in every way, whether in pretense or in truth, Christ is proclaimed, and in that I rejoice. Yes, and I will rejoice. (vv. 12–18)

We learn a number of lessons from Paul's words here.

1. Contentment comes by turning our afflictions into mercies.

First, contentment in affliction comes by recognizing how God is working in our hardship. When we do this, we see our afflictions not as setbacks or as inconveniences. Rather, they are mercies from God.

Paul makes clear that in his imprisonment, not only has the gospel not been hindered, but it has actually advanced. First, the gospel is preached among the palace guard. This guard was an elite group of soldiers who had important and prestigious assignments and typically received double pay. Paul's imprisonment provided him a unique opportunity to reach these elite soldiers for Christ—and through them to reach others ("and to all the rest," 1:13).

In addition, Paul's imprisonment emboldened others to preach the gospel fearlessly. Believers rose up to preach Christ during Paul's time of confinement. Far from being intimidated by Paul's circumstances, they gained courage and did what Paul could not do.

As an aside, this pattern has been repeated in the church throughout history. Several years ago a missionary named Chet Bitterman, a Wycliffe Bible translator in Colombia, was taken prisoner by a guerrilla group and was held for seven weeks. He was eventually shot and killed. Were other Christians deterred from entering missionary work? To the contrary, Wycliffe reported that in the following year applications for overseas ministry doubled. The church father Tertullian has famously said, "The blood of martyrs is the seed of the church."[1] God has continually raised up from the ashes of affliction a mighty army to achieve his purposes.

It is one thing, however, to recognize that God works through hardship and tragedy. It is quite another to look at our own afflictions and to see them as mercies from God. But this is the perspective we need.

Hebrews 12 exhorts us to receive hardship as God's discipline. This passage has much to teach us about God's sovereignty. The hardship in mind is persecution, which clearly comes from wicked, unbelieving men. Yet the writer to the Hebrews also treats it as coming from God, disciplining his children, treating them as a father treats his beloved sons.

The fact that trials come both from sinful men and from God is difficult for us to understand. But it is consistent with biblical teaching. Joseph's brothers hated him, mistreated him, and sold him into slavery. Yet, while not condoning their sinful actions, Joseph could still see God as the author: "you meant evil against me, but God meant it for good" (Gen. 50:20).

An important part of turning our afflictions into mercies is developing a vision of God's sovereignty in all things, recognizing that God does all things for his glory and for our spiritual good. In one of the most poignant passages in John Calvin's writings, he reflects on the death of his son. After describing his grief, Calvin says of God, "But he is our Father; he knows what is best for his children."[2]

This is part of the mystery of contentment. It differs radically from worldly thinking. The world says that contentment comes by finding release from afflictions. The Christian finds contentment in the midst of afflictions, by turning them into mercies. The point is not that we go looking for hardship and revel in our trials. Christianity is no friend of masochism. But when suffering comes, we recognize the hand of God at work and see his mercies in the midst of it.

Charles Spurgeon told the story of a well-known painter working on a high platform in St. Paul's Cathedral. He was examining his work, backing up inch by inch to take in the whole. Suddenly his feet were at the very edge of the platform. One of his assistants noticed this. He did not cry out for fear that it would startle the painter or cause him to look back and so fall to his death. Thinking quickly, he grabbed a paint brush, dipped it in paint, and flung it on the artist's work. This enraged the painter, and he came forward to confront his assistant. Only then did he recognize that the ruin of his work had meant the saving of his life.[3]

Our afflictions are God's mercies.

2. Contentment comes by performing the work of our circumstances.

Second, we learn from Paul's own example in Philippians 1:12ff. that contentment comes by performing the work of our circumstances. Paul says, "it has become known throughout the whole imperial guard and to all the rest that my imprisonment is for Christ" (v. 13). How has it become known among the imperial guard that Paul's imprisonment is for Christ? The answer is, Paul made it known to them. He continued to preach Christ in his imprisonment.

Paul could have seen his imprisonment as a setback to his mission to take the gospel to the ends of the world. He could have sat back, prayed, and waited to be released so that his "real" ministry could resume. Instead he recognized his imprisonment as an opportunity. He performed the work of his circumstances.

In a recent survey people were asked the question, "What do you live for?" Ninety-four percent responded that they were waiting for something to take place. There were a variety of things that people were waiting for—waiting to get married, waiting to get a good job, waiting for a new job, waiting to have kids, waiting for the kids to grow up, etc. But the predominant answer was that people live their lives waiting for something else.

The question the contented Christian asks is, what is the duty of my present circumstances? And carrying out that duty is vital both to Christian faithfulness and to Christian contentment. Maybe we are not where we want to be. There is nothing sinful about desiring and praying for difficult circumstances to change. But we need to seek how we can serve Christ where we are.

John Newton writes,

> If two angels were to receive at the same moment a commission from God, one to go down and rule earth's grandest empire, the other to go and sweep the streets of its meanest village, it would be a matter of entire indifference to each which service fell to his lot, the post of ruler or the post of scavenger; for the joy of angels lies only in obedience to God's will.[4]

This secret of contentment is radically different from the thinking of sinful man. The sinful heart says, "Get me into a situation in which I can be content." The Christian pursuing sanctification and contentment says, "Help me to be content in this situation and to perform the duty of it."

We need to remember that contentment comes by the grace and power of God within us. Contentment is the result of a transformed heart. It is not tied to external circumstances.

It is well known that the divorce rate in America has for years hovered around 50 percent. But statistics tell us that the divorce rate for second marriages is much higher than that (at least 60 percent, if not pushing 70 percent), and the statistics for third marriages is even higher. We often get the impression that when a situation is bad, the solution is to get out of it. If we are in a bad marriage, we need to get out and get into a better one. The problem, of course, is that we take our problems with us. Moving from one situation to the next is typically not the solution to our hardships.

Burroughs uses the illustration of children who climb a hill, thinking they will be able to reach the clouds. When they get to the top, they realize that the clouds are too far above to reach them. But they see another hill in the distance and think, *If only we could get to the top of that hill, we would be able to touch the clouds.*

So it is with us. We are tempted to think, *If only my circumstances changed, I would be content.* But often the situation does change, and we still are discontented. Our focus must be on what God has called us to do now, where he has currently placed us.

I once heard Sandy Willson, pastor of Second Presbyterian Church in Memphis, say that 90 percent of those who come for pastoral counseling today seek relief from their suffering. On the other hand, one hundred years ago 90 percent of those seeking pastoral counseling came to get help to serve God in the midst of their suffering. They sought to discover the duty of their present circumstances and to fulfill it. In other words, they followed the example of Paul, as well as of Christ and all of the great persecuted saints in the Bible.

3. Contentment comes by melting our will and desires into Christ's will and desires.

Third, contentment in affliction comes by melting our will and desires into Christ's will and desires. Hardship typically leaves us preoccupied with our own difficulties. When we are self-absorbed, our focus remains on our troubles and on finding release from them. While afflicted and centered on ourselves, discontentment is the inevitable result. Thus we need to learn to give over our will and desires to Christ and to be ruled by his will and his desires.

Paul serves as a great example of that here in Philippians 1. In verses 15–18, Paul expounds on those who have been emboldened by his imprisonment to preach Christ. These preachers have different motivations. Some preach Christ from goodwill and love, taking up Paul's ministry because they know that he is in prison for the defense of the gospel. But others preach Christ out of envy and rivalry, even seeking to add to Paul's afflictions in prison.

We do not know for sure who these rival preachers were or why they were seeking to add to Paul's afflictions. Perhaps they were embarrassed by Paul's imprisonment. Maybe they wanted to usurp his authority. Paul clearly does not condone their motives. Their motives are evil.

Yet Paul rejoices because Christ is being preached. Certainly Paul's desire would be not to face this affliction and not to have these preachers who have set themselves up against him. But Paul does not fret about these preachers, their motives, or the affliction they have added to him. Rather, he melts his will into Christ's. The greater good is the glory of Christ. Christ is being preached, and Paul is content with that.

We need to pray for the grace to be content in knowing that God's will is being done despite our circumstances.

This requires the development of a God-centered, Christ-centered vision, a vision that is antithetical to the predominant ways of thinking in today's evangelical subculture. I was recently riding in the car with my twelve-year-old daughter, listening to her CD of the past year's greatest hits in Christian music. From beginning to end, the songs were I- or me-focused: "I want to feel you," "wrap your arms around me," one even asking Christ (I assume) to "kiss me."

So I entered into a discussion with her about the music. Much was good in the music, so I did not discourage her from listening to it. But I did tell her simply to be aware of music that focuses so much on my own personal experience as opposed to being God- or Christ-centered. There is nothing wrong with expressing my own experience or desires. The Psalms often speak in the first person singular. But the Psalms also more significantly teach us to turn our gaze away from self and to the sovereign plans and purposes of God.

Psalm 73 is a wonderful example of this. The psalmist's "feet had almost stumbled," his "steps had nearly slipped" (v. 2). He envied the wicked for their prosperity and their seemingly trouble-free life. He complains, "All in vain have I kept my heart clean and washed my hands in innocence. For all the day long I have been stricken and rebuked every morning"

(vv. 13–14). He was consumed with fretting, contrasting his situation to that of the rich oppressors. This continued "until I went into the sanctuary of God; then I discerned their end" (v. 17). In the sanctuary, his vision became God-focused, and he began to see God's purposes and plans. His desires melted into God's desires, and his troubled spirit found peace.

This psalm is instructive because it indicates to us that there is a time to register our complaints and to relate the experiences of our souls. But contentment comes only when we look away from self and rest in God's sovereign control.

The great Reformer Martin Luther experienced the death of his daughter Magdalena. Roland Bainton records Luther's grief as follows:

> When Magdalena was fourteen years old, she lay upon her deathbed. Luther prayed, "O God, I love her so, but thy will be done." And turning to her, "*Magdalenchen*, my little girl, you would like to stay with your father here and you would be glad to go to your Father in heaven?"
>
> And she said, "Yes, dear father, as God wills."
>
> And Luther reproached himself because God had blessed him as no bishop had been blessed in a thousand years, and yet he could not find it in his heart to give God thanks. Katie [his wife] stood off, overcome by grief; and Luther held the child in his arms as she passed on. When she was laid away, he said, "*Du liebes Lenchen*, you will rise and shine like the stars and the sun. How strange it is to know that she is at peace and all is well, and yet to be so sorrowful!"[5]

This passage vividly describes Luther's struggle with his own pain and sorrow. Yet at the same time we see his recognition of the superior plans of God and of God's goodness in the midst of his grief. Contentment does not mean that we face life without pain. It *does* mean that in the midst of our affliction we are able to find peace in God's sovereign control, melting our will into his.

4. Contentment comes by seeking the good of others in the midst of our affliction.

Fourth, contentment comes by seeking the good of others, even in the midst of our affliction. When we stop and look at the larger picture of Philippians 1:12–18, it becomes clear that Paul is writing this section to comfort and reassure the Philippians. They have concerns about his situation. They are experiencing distress. But Paul writes here to tell them that God has everything under control. They need not worry about him.

We especially see the heart of Paul in verses 19–26 where Paul is contemplating his own future, especially with regard to his present imprisonment. Will it end in death or release? We see his greatest desire in verse 20—that, whether in life or death, Christ will be honored in his body. But then we also see two warring desires. One is to carry on his ministry in this life. The other is to depart and to be with Christ, which, Paul says, "is far better" (v. 23). Ultimately he is willing to let go of that personal desire for the good of the Philippians. For their progress in the faith, it is more necessary that he remain in the flesh (vv. 24–26).

Paul's consuming passion was for the glory of Christ and the spiritual good of those under his care. Time after time his ministry confirms this. His contentment comes from having a heart that beats for others. A minister friend of mine once said that when he gets down and discouraged, he goes to visit and minister to others. These visits turn him outward and keep him from becoming preoccupied with his own concerns.

Those who have been in the ministry can testify to the numerous times when they have gone to comfort dying saints and they themselves have left encouraged and uplifted by the faith and testimony of the other. The afflicted saint often becomes a source of comfort and encouragement to others.

Charles Simeon was pastor of Trinity Church in Cambridge, England for fifty-four years. He faced many hardships in his life, including initial rejection by the congregation. For twelve years they locked their pews, and Simeon was forced to preach to those standing in the aisles and around the back of the sanctuary. Simeon died after a long and difficult battle with illness. Three weeks before his death some of his own people gathered around his bed. These are his recorded words on that occasion:

> Infinite wisdom has arranged the whole with infinite love. And infinite power enables me to rest upon that love. I am in the dear Father's hands. All is secure. When I look to him I see nothing but faithfulness and immutability and truth. And I have the sweetest peace. I cannot have more peace.[6]

In the midst of his struggle, Simeon encouraged those around him by his unshakable faith in the sovereignty, love, and goodness of God.

We can add one final point that seems to be implicit in Paul's testimony, as it is in the testimonies of other suffering saints. To have contentment in suffering we must recognize and actively remind ourselves of the goodness of God in the midst of our affliction. God is a loving Father who cares for his children. God does not promise us a trouble-free life. God even afflicts his children as he sees fit. Yet in the end we must remember that God is good and that he works for the good of his children.

Christians throughout the ages have found great comfort in Romans 8:28: "And we know that for those who love God all things work together for good, for those who are called according to his purpose." "*All things* work together for good." Does that mean even suffering and hardship? The larger context of Romans 8 reveals that this is precisely what it means.

In Romans 8:17 Paul says that we are "fellow heirs with Christ, provided we suffer with him in order that we may also be glorified with him." As verse 18 indicates, the entire following section is a reflection on "the sufferings of this present time." In this age, believers, as well as all of creation, groan, waiting for final redemption (v. 23). Present life, then, is a mixture of both suffering and hope (v. 24). The Spirit's activity, helping us in our weakness (vv. 26–27), is a source of hope. But ultimately the believer's hope is rooted in God's work—predestining, calling, justifying, glorifying (vv. 29–30).

Romans 8 concludes, then, with a glorious section proclaiming that God is for us, that the One who did not spare his own Son will freely give us all things, and that nothing can separate us from the love of God in Christ Jesus. But all of this is affirmed against the backdrop of present sufferings:

> Who shall separate us from the love of Christ? Shall tribulation, or distress, or persecution, or famine, or nakedness, or

danger, or sword? As it is written, "For your sake we are being killed all the day long; we are regarded as sheep to be slaughtered." No, in all these things we are more than conquerors through him who loved us. (vv. 35–37)

It is within this larger context that Paul makes his statement in Romans 8:28 that all things work together for good for those who love God.

The question is, do we believe that? Do we believe that our hardships, our suffering, our pain works together for good for those who love God? "Good," of course, does not mean easy or painless. But God's purposes are for our spiritual good, whatever may be our physical or emotional path.

The seventeenth-century hymn "Whate'er My God Ordains Is Right" perfectly captures the essence of this biblical truth.

Whate'er my God ordains is right:
   His holy will abideth;
I will be still whate'er he doth,
   And follow where he guideth:
He is my God; Though dark my road,
   He holds me that I shall not fall:
Wherefore to him I leave it all.

Whate'er my God ordains is right:
   He never will deceive me;
He leads me by the proper path;
   I know he will not leave me:
I take, content, What he hath sent;
   His hand can turn my griefs away,
And patiently I wait his day.

Whate'er my God ordains is right:
 Though now this cup, in drinking,
May bitter seem to my faint heart,
 I take it, all unshrinking:
My God is true; Each morn anew
 Sweet comfort yet shall fill my heart,
And pain and sorrow shall depart.

Whate'er my God ordains is right:
 Here shall my stand be taken;
Though sorrow, need, or death be mine,
 Yet am I not forsaken;
My Father's care Is round me there;
 He holds me that I shall not fall:
And so to him I leave it all.[7]

God is good. God is faithful. God is for us. This is the consistent biblical message. Be content in your affliction.

Discussion Questions

1. How important is it to develop the perspective that afflictions and suffering are inevitable? Why?

2. As you look back on your life to this point, can you think of specific times of hardship or disappointments that you later recognized as mercies from God? How can we develop this perspective in the midst of our trials?

3. Do you agree that suffering can be both from sinful man and from God for our good? Many people assert that God "allows" suffering but does not bring suffering because

suffering is an evil and God cannot do what is evil. How would you respond to this?

4. How do we draw the line between recognizing the good that God brings through suffering and developing a masochistic attitude that takes pleasure in suffering?

5. Can you think of those in your own experience who suffered greatly, yet continually sought the will of Christ and served him through their suffering? Stop and pray for God's grace to follow in their footsteps.

CHAPTER 6

The Mathematics of Contentment

✠

WHEN I WAS GROWING UP, I heard a lot of talk about what was called "the new math." To be honest, I never quite learned what "the new math" was. I heard the jokes—"In the new math, one plus one equals three." But I was trained in conservative schools, and the old math worked fine for us. The new math seems to have been based on new ways of thinking about reality. It was a new approach, a new way of looking at the world, rooted in new scientific assumptions.

For a Christian to find true contentment, he must begin to see life and reality in a new way. Contentment is the result of some "new math"—adding and subtracting not according to the predominant worldly paradigm but according to biblical teaching. The world has its own formulas for happiness. Typically the world and the sinful heart say, "If you want true happiness, you need to add things and reduce burdens." Sometimes the world says, "If you want to find happiness, you must subtract things and live more simply."

But neither of these approaches is biblical. Scripture teaches a different formula for adding and subtracting that enables us to learn contentment.

If we want to learn contentment, we must learn God's new math. Contentment comes by addition and subtraction.

1. Contentment by addition—adding a new burden to our current burdens.

First, contentment comes by addition—namely, not getting rid of the burden of our situation but adding a new one. This seems like a strange proposition. Why would we want to add another burden to our current burden? In fact, our desire is typically to want to be rid of our burdens altogether.

But there is a burden that it is right for Christians to bear, and this burden puts all of our other burdens in perspective. In particular, Christians should in a sense bear the burden of their sin. Our sin should grieve us. We should be overwhelmed by its horror and by the fact that every sin is an offense against a holy God.

Proverbs tells us that the fear of God is the beginning of wisdom. While this fear is not the fear of final judgment or rejection, at the very least it is the fear of God's displeasure. The cause of this displeasure is certainly our sin. It is right, then, as well as wise, to be troubled by our sin.

One of the most controversial aspects of Puritan and traditional Reformed thought is an introspective conscience that is burdened by the weight of sin. Those who object to this argue, first, that our guilt has been removed by the death of Christ and God has put our sin as far from us as the east is from the west. Therefore, Christians should not bear the burden of something that Christ has taken away. He bore our burden so we would not have to.

A second objection to an introspective conscience is that instead of being inward focused, we need to look outward. We need to focus our attention on serving other Christians or serving the world in evangelism and mercy ministries. Christians who carry the burden of their sin will be ineffective in meeting the needs around them, or so the argument goes.

Both of these objections, however, fail to represent a full-orbed view of the reality of the Christian life. On the one hand, while it is true that Christ bore the guilt of our sin and has broken the power of sin's tyrannical reign over us, it is also true that Christians remain sinners. It is right to recognize and grieve over remaining sin. The apostle John, in his first epistle, recognizes that God has sent Christ to be the propitiation for our sins (1 John 2:1–2). At the same time, he exhorts Christians to recognize their sin and to confess it, as a result of which God forgives them and cleanses them from unrighteousness (1 John 1:8–10).

On the other hand, an inward focus and an outward one are not mutually exclusive. Both are important aspects of the Christian life. In fact, those who know their own sin and their own neediness are best equipped to minister to the sins and needs of others.

The classic New Testament passage dealing with the ongoing reality and grief of sin is Romans 7. Though justified (Rom. 5:1) and already made a slave of righteousness (Rom. 6:15–23), Paul recognizes that sin still dwells within him. He does what he does not want to do and does not do the thing he desires to do. Sin still has a foothold, even if its power has been broken. The weight of this sin even leads Paul to declare himself a "wretched man" (7:24).[1]

Paul can hardly be accused either of not understanding the reality of new life in Christ, that sin's guilt and sin's power no longer rule the Christian, or of being so introspective that he fails to serve others or witness for Christ. Yet Paul still is burdened by his sin. Romans 7 epitomizes the believer's struggle with and attitude toward indwelling sin.

It should not be surprising, then, that Paul is contented and refuses to be burdened by external circumstances. The burden of sin swallows up the weight of all other burdens in our life. If we want to be less burdened by our circumstances, we need to become more burdened by our sin.

What is the most difficult situation that we face in our lives? We might be tempted to say things like finding out we have cancer, facing the death of a loved one or child, or some other terrible, life-changing situation. But the reality is that the most troublesome situation of life, according to Scripture, is to be in a state that is displeasing to God. What we should seek to avoid at all costs is not affliction or want. Rather, it is disobedience to God in willful sin.

If this is true, then the burden of our sin puts all other burdens in proper perspective. If sin is our greatest burden, all other burdens are made lighter.

This is quite different from the typical response of the natural self. The unbeliever, or the worldly man, asks, "Why should we add burdens to our lives? Instead we should lighten our load." In fact, popular slogans in our culture reflect this kind of attitude. "Chill out," "Be happy," "Whatever!"—these all reflect a desire for an easygoing attitude that refuses to be burdened by *anything*. This is especially true of the world's attitude toward sin.

But this response to the burdens of life does not adequately deal with them. The burdens always return.

The Christian response to affliction must include self-examination. Heart-searching self-examination produces one of three things: First, the Christian might conclude that a single sin or sin pattern is the cause of affliction. We must be careful because the Bible clearly indicates that not all human affliction is the direct result of a specific sin that a person has committed. Think of Job and the blind man in John 9 (cf. v. 3). At the same time, some of our affliction is the result of sin. Paul's teaching on the abuses at the Lord's Supper in Corinth is a clear example of this (1 Cor. 11:27–32). When we see our sin, we must repent of it and rest in the mercy of God to bring relief from our affliction when and if he sees fit.

Second, when the Christian examines himself, he may recognize in himself the sin of discontent. Again, he must repent of this sin and ask God to bring contentment in the midst of affliction.

Third, when a Christian looks deeply at his life and the idols of his heart, it puts his entire situation in proper spiritual perspective. It reminds him that sin, not his circumstance, is the greatest enemy. The burden, the affliction, the external circumstance suddenly loses its controlling power in our lives. Recognizing the burden of sin lessens the other burdens in our life.

When affliction hits a family, whether it be money problems, relational problems, loss of a job, or death of a child, often the result is discontent and strife. In fact, many marriages seem to be fine until trouble hits, resulting in seemingly unbearable conflict. This may lead a husband and wife to say that it is not good to live together in the strife. But what is the best solution? Simply this: humble yourselves and confess your sins to God and to one another. Humility and acknowledgment of sin enable couples to ride out the storm.

In the same way, when afflictions come, humility and recognition of sin put us in the best position to endure the hardship. If you want contentment, examine your heart and be weighed down by your sin.

2. Contentment by subtraction—making our desires equal to our circumstances.

Second, contentment comes not just by addition, but also by subtraction. A popular worldly philosophy says the way to find true contentment and peace is by subtracting from our circumstances and getting rid of things. But this is of no value in the pursuit of contentment if our hearts are not changed.

Proper biblical subtraction, however, is vital for contentment. To find contentment we must subtract from desires so that our desires and our circumstances are even and equal. This is the reason that so many who have less than others are content in their circumstances. Having little does not itself produce contentment. Rather, they are content because God has fashioned their hearts to their circumstances.

The fact that this gift comes from God, however, does not mean we play no part in the process. We can and must do several things as we pursue contentment in this way. First and foremost, we need to pray. We need to pray that God will give us proper desires, and we must confess improper desires to God. We need to ask God to give us a heart fashioned to our circumstances, instead of giving us what we want to bring our circumstances up to our desires.

Second, we need to guard our hearts. Solomon warns his son, "Watch over your heart with all diligence, for from it *flow* the springs of life" (Prov. 4:23 NASB). We have a responsibility to keep our desires in check and to root out those desires that are improper. Again, meditating on the tenth commandment is vital. Are our hearts ruled by covetousness?

Third, we need to watch what we let into our minds and hearts. Advertisements, shopping channels, and other media can inflame, not lessen, the desires of our hearts. Recently I bought a new car. My previous, fifteen-year-old model was shot. I had put several hundred dollars of repair into it, and several more hundred dollars of repair were needed soon—and there was no end in sight. So I began to look in the newspaper and on the Internet to research cars. I ended up buying a relatively cheap economy model. But the experience whetted my appetite for more. For weeks afterward I asked myself, *Why didn't I buy such-and-such?* I was addicted to the automotive pages and fantasized about "my next car." I learned that I needed to stay away from those pages in the newspaper. They only made me want more, not to be satisfied with what God gave me.

Instead of matching desires to circumstances, the world seeks to bring its circumstances up to its desires. But the Bible teaches that this is inherently dangerous. Paul warns Timothy, "those who desire to be rich fall into temptation, into a snare, into many senseless and harmful desires that plunge people into ruin and destruction" (1 Tim. 6:9). In a similar vein, Ecclesiastes 5:10 teaches, "He who loves money will not be satisfied with money, nor he who loves wealth with his income." Seeking to raise our circumstances to our desires is simply a chasing after the wind.

To use a rather grotesque illustration, imagine a man with one very long leg and one short leg. He would have a difficult time walking. In fact, he would not get along nearly as well as a man with two short legs. His legs are of little use to him because they are not even.

This is exactly the situation of a person whose desires are beyond his circumstances. He may be poor or he may be rich, but if his desires are for more, his spiritual walk with Christ is hindered. On the other hand, one of low circumstance with equal desires walks with ease.

3. Contentment by subtraction—rooting out ungodly desires.

Third, contentment also comes from subtraction in the sense of purging what is within that displeases God. A contented Christian is one who has done radical internal surgery to root out the evil desires in his heart. Again, this is contrary to the carnal mind. The carnal mind says that to acquire contentment we must get something from the outside. But biblical contentment comes only by getting out what is within that hinders contentment.

Remember, contentment is an inward attribute. It is not tied to externals. Precisely because it is internal we must get rid of those things within us that hinder our contentment. The Christian is engaged in a battle for the heart and soul. Certainly we battle for the heart and soul of those who do not know Christ. But this battle begins within the Christian himself.

The greatest servants the church has produced have known this battle. Henry Martyn, the great missionary to India, wrote powerfully of the warfare of the soul. He described his boat trip to India as follows:

> I found it hard to realize divine things. I was more tried with desires after the world, than for two years past. . . . The seasickness, and the smell of the ship, made me feel very miserable, and the prospect of leaving all the comforts and communion of saints in England, to go forth to an unknown land, to endure such illness and misery with ungodly men for so many months, weighed heavy on my spirits. My heart was almost ready to break.[2]

Missionaries in particular must battle with their desires for the familiar and the comfortable as they leave home to go to places and callings that will inevitably bring hardship.

But the battle is no less real for the Christian who does the work of God where he is. There is always a longing for comfort, for wealth, for status and prestige. The struggle against desire for things of this world is constant. Of course, many Christians do not struggle but simply give in to the world and the desires of the heart. But they will never attain contentment. The desires that wage war with our soul must be purged.

James tells us that the cause of quarrels and fights is within (James 4:1–5). Interestingly, the warring outside is a symptom of the warring that takes place inside: "What causes quarrels and what causes fights among you? Is it not this, that your passions are at war within you?" (v. 1). He then goes on to describe the nature of this war within and what it leads to: "You desire and do not have, so you murder. You covet and cannot obtain, so you fight and quarrel" (v. 2). The Christian who desires the things of the world is a friend of the world—and therefore an enemy of God (vv. 4–5).

The experience of battling desires (as well as battling Christians!) is common. But James's solution is uncompromising: "Cleanse your hands, you sinners, and purify your hearts, you double-minded" (4:8). In other words, purge the evil desires from within you. Without doing so, there simply can be no peace.

This is fully in line with biblical teaching elsewhere about mortification. Paul writes, "Put to death therefore what is earthly in you: sexual immorality, impurity, passion, evil desire, and covetousness, which is idolatry" (Col. 3:5). The Christian is not to foster evil desire or treat it lightly. He must ruthlessly mortify—or put to death—the lusts and impure passions within him.

President Ronald Reagan popularized the slogan, "Peace through strength." For the Christian, peace comes only through the battle to purge the sins and idols of the heart.

In a sense we have come full circle in this study. We began by saying that we overcome covetousness by learning contentment. At the same time we acquire contentment only by putting covetousness to death. The mathematics of contentment requires this type of subtraction.

Discussion Questions

1. Is it proper for the Christian to be burdened by the weight of his sin? Have you had times when God has revealed to

you, through godly introspection, sins of the heart? Does your experience with sin match that of the apostle Paul in Romans 7?

2. Do you agree that being burdened by sin helps put other burdens in perspective and can lead to godly contentment? Why or why not? How does this experience of being burdened by sin differ from the philosophy of the world?

3. Reflect on your own experience with your desires. Have you had times when the desire for something has led to further, unquenchable desires? Have the things of this world ever truly satisfied you? What are some practical steps that you can take to begin to bring your desires down to meet your present circumstances?

4. What sinful desires are the most prominent in your heart? What do you need to do to begin to mortify—that is, put to death—those sinful desires?

CHAPTER 7

The Contentment of Longing for Heaven

❖

FLORENCE CHADWICK was a famous and accomplished swimmer. She was the first woman to swim the English Channel both ways. In 1952 she attempted to swim from Catalina Island to the shore of mainland California. On the day she set out, the weather was so foggy that she could barely see the boats that accompanied her.

She swam for fifteen hours and was exhausted. She asked to be taken out of the water, but she was told that the shore was not far away. Those accompanying her exhorted her to continue. "You can make it," they pleaded. But finally she just gave up and was pulled out of the water. She was too exhausted to go on. But when she was taken out, she discovered that the shore was only half a mile away.

Later she told a reporter, "Look, I'm not excusing myself. But if I could have seen land, I might have made it." Two months later she did, becoming the first woman to make the swim and breaking the record for the fastest time.[1]

The contented Christian also must keep his or her eyes on the goal and ultimate destination—namely, heaven. Heaven is our safe haven. The thought of heaven keeps the believer pressing forward. But even more than that, the contented Christian is one who longs for heaven.

This seems contradictory. Isn't the contented person the one who truly is at home in this world? Isn't the essence of contentment to find peace here, not longing for something that is still to come? To the contrary, the Bible teaches that contentment only comes when we recognize that this world is not our home. In this life heaven is found in the one who longs for heaven.

A return to Philippians helps us see how Paul's reflections on and desires for heaven contributed to his attaining contentment. Prior to Paul's description of his contentment (Phil. 4:11–13), he makes two crucial statements about the outlook of the Christian. We will look at these in the reverse order in which Paul presents them. First, Paul instructs believers that their citizenship is in heaven (3:20). Second, Paul describes his greatest desire as being to depart and be with Christ (1:23).

1. The contented Christian recognizes that his citizenship is in heaven.

The apostle Paul writes, "But our citizenship is in heaven, and from it we await a Savior, the Lord Jesus Christ" (Phil. 3:20). The notion of citizenship was an important one to the Philippians. The city of Philippi was a Roman colony and had all the privileges of special status with Rome. The citizens of Philippi were Roman citizens, and the city valued its favored position. Philippi modeled itself in many respects on Rome, such that many have referred to it as a "miniature Rome."

It is significant, then, that Paul uses the language of citizenship twice in this letter. The first comes in 1:27 where he literally exhorts the Philippian Christians to "live as citizens" in a manner worthy of the gospel. The second is the passage quoted above.

In contrast to the attitude in Philippi, which cherished its Roman citizenship, the Philippian Christians were to recognize their heavenly citizenship. The unbeliever sets his entire hope on this world and values life in the world above all. But the Christian recognizes that he is a pilgrim and alien in this world (1 Peter 2:11). His true home is in heaven.

Bible-believing Christians have sometimes been accused of being "so heavenly-minded that they are no earthly good." But we can give two responses to this. First, as Scottish preacher Eric Alexander has simply stated it, "Never in all my years of ministry have I met a person who is 'too heavenly-minded.' " In fact, we are earthly-minded. We are consumed by life in this world. We don't need a self-help book on how to stay focused on the things of the present age. It is difficult to find those who are truly heavenly-minded.

Second, we can make the case from Scripture that the more heavenly-minded we are, the more useful we become on earth. The apostle Paul exhorted the Colossians, "Set your minds on things that are above, not on things that are on earth" (Col. 3:2). This serves as the foundation for his later ethical instructions to put sin to death (3:5ff.), to live together in love and unity (3:12ff.), and to fulfill our obligations in the home and at work (3:18–4:1). The earthly-minded are consumed with self-seeking. The heavenly-minded seek the things of God, which translates into living with one another and serving one another in godly ways.

Paul also reveals his heavenly-minded bent in Philippians 1 when he tells of his own desire to depart and to be with Christ, a passage that we will return to below. But it is this desire that compels him to further ministry. As Paul states it, "for me to live is Christ," and this leads him to live for others, even as Christ did (cf. Phil. 1:21–26; 2:5–11).

The Christian who recognizes that his citizenship is in heaven (Phil. 3:20) is the one who "lives as a citizen" worthy of the gospel (Phil. 1:27). Heavenly values determine his life. He rejects the thinking of the world. In this way he becomes especially useful on earth.

Jeremiah Burroughs, in a different work than the one that has been the focus of this study, writes as follows:

> This will be the difference between men and women at the day of judgment for, the truth is, what is this world but a seafare? We are sailing in this world, with either a load of pearls, or with that which has no worth at all. When you live in the times of the gospel, there is a market for pearls, for those things that will enrich you to all eternity. One man bestows all the strength of his thoughts and heart on those things for which he shall be blessing God in the highest heavens to all eternity, and the other bestows his thoughts and heart on the things of the earth, loading himself down with thick clay. There is a man or woman that shall be blessed for all of eternity, that shall join with angels and saints in the highest heavens to magnify the free grace of God in Christ.

And there is another that, had he bestowed his thoughts and heart on the same things, he might have been blessed forever also, but he, minding the things of the earth, is a cursed fool and is the scorn and contempt of men and angels to all eternity.[2]

Whether we are heavenly- or earthly-minded affects what we value—pearls or worthless clay—and therefore how we live.

Furthermore, the thought of heaven contents the Christian. The fears, restless rushing, and turmoil of this life do not overwhelm him. He remains peaceful in the midst of the storm. The reason for this is simply that glory awaits him, an eternity without fear, sin, and death. Burroughs states, "there is a heaven in the soul of a godly man." He continues, "no soul shall ever come to heaven, but the soul which has heaven come to it first."[3]

Simply put, there is no godliness (and therefore no contentment) without heavenly-mindedness.

2. The contented Christian longs to depart and be with Christ; yet he carries on the work that Christ has given him to do.

In Philippians 1:23 Paul states, "My desire is to depart and be with Christ, for that is far better." It is one thing to recognize that our citizenship is in heaven. It is another thing to long to be there. Paul desires to depart this life and to be with Christ. This is vital both to his attainment of contentment and to his self-giving service to Christ's church. His deepest desires for heaven determine his present life on earth.

It is important to see the flow of Paul's thought in Philippians 1:18–26. Many English translations correctly begin a new paragraph with the last part of verse 18, "Yes, and I will rejoice." Verses 19–26, then, explain this opening statement. We have already seen that joy/rejoicing and contentment are closely related in Philippians. Thus, this entire paragraph describes for us how Paul attains this contentment.

> Yes, and I will rejoice, for I know that through your prayers and the help of the Spirit of Jesus Christ this will turn out for my deliverance, as it is my eager expectation and hope that I will not be at all ashamed, but that with full courage now as always Christ will be honored in my body, whether by life or by death. For to me to live is Christ, and to die is gain. If I am to live in the flesh, that means fruitful labor for me. Yet which I shall choose I cannot tell. I am hard pressed between the two. My desire is to depart and be with Christ, for that is far better. But to remain in the flesh is more necessary on your account. Convinced of this, I know that I will remain and continue with you all, for your progress and joy in the faith, so that in me you may have ample cause to glory in Christ Jesus, because of my coming to you again. (Phil. 1:18b–26)

The relationship between verse 18b ("yes, and I will rejoice") and verses 19–26 is made clear by a series of explanatory clauses. Two of these clauses begin with the word "for" (vv. 19 and 21), giving a further explanation of what Paul has just said. Verses 22–26 expound Paul's statement in verse 21 ("For to me to live is Christ, and to die is gain"). Thus the entire paragraph is tightly and carefully constructed to detail the source of Paul's joy. Let's trace the flow of his thought here.

Paul follows his opening affirmation, "Yes, and I will rejoice," with an explanatory "for" clause: "for . . . this will turn out for my deliverance" (v. 19). The word translated "deliverance" in the ESV is Paul's normal word for "salvation," and this is probably its sense here. Paul rejoices because he knows that even his current situation in prison, with others stirring up hardship for him in his chains (vv. 12–18), will eventually, through the Philippians' prayers and the help of the Holy Spirit, lead to his salvation.

This confidence, furthermore, is in line with Paul's hope and expectation that he will not be ashamed, but that Christ will be exalted in his body (v. 20). Paul is apparently reflecting on his own faithfulness here. Will he remain faithful to the end? He recognizes that he cannot do so in his own power. He needs the Spirit's help. He needs their prayers. Ultimately, then, Christ, not Paul, is exalted. And this exaltation of Christ will take place whether Paul lives or dies.

Verse 21 follows with another explanatory "for" clause: "For to me to live is Christ, and to die is gain." In other words, life for Paul is all about Christ. Life now is Christ; death is gain because it means more of Christ. That is why Paul can say that Christ will be honored whether he lives or dies (v. 20). If he goes on living, he will seek to exalt Christ. If he dies, Christ is exalted in Paul's faithfulness to Christ.

This in turn affects how Paul views his life in this world. If he continues in the flesh, it will mean "fruitful labor" for him (v. 22). Furthermore, the fact that life is Christ leads Paul to view his life in terms of what is best for his churches (vv. 23–26).

Though his deepest desire is to depart and be with Christ, he recognizes that it is more necessary currently that he remain in this world and continue to labor on behalf of the church. And so he chooses to make this his current preference. Ultimately it is the Christ-centered nature of Paul's life and desires that lead to his commitment to faithful service on earth.

We see, then, that Paul's rejoicing and contentment are ultimately rooted in his eschatology—that is, in his view of what is to come. He rejoices because his present circumstances will turn out for his salvation, meaning that Christ will be exalted whether he lives or dies. And it will turn out this way precisely because for him to live is Christ and to die is gain. His hope for the future gives him a sense of peace with regard to how this life will turn out. He faces life—and therefore death!—with confidence.

But at a deeper level Paul's peace and contentment are ultimately found in his relationship and communion with Christ. Life is Christ and death is gain precisely because they both mean more of Christ. It is the intimacy and satisfaction that Paul has with Christ now that leads him to say that he longs to depart and to be with Christ. He desires to see Christ face-to-face. He longs for greater intimacy and a stronger bond of communion that only comes when the Christian completes his life in the world. Far from being afraid to die, Paul longed for it because it meant more of Christ.

The hymn "The Sands of Time Are Sinking," based on writings of Samuel Rutherford, beautifully captures this truth. Verse 1 expresses a desire for heaven in light of the trials of this life. But verses 2–4 focus on the true joy of heaven—Christ himself.

The sands of time are sinking,
The dawn of heaven breaks,
The summer morn I've sighed for,
The fair sweet morn awakes;
Dark, dark, hath been the midnight,
But dayspring is at hand,
And glory, glory dwelleth
In Emmanuel's land.

The King there in his beauty
Without a veil is seen;
It were a well-spent journey
Though seven deaths lay between:
The Lamb with his fair army
Doth on Mount Zion stand,
And glory, glory dwelleth
In Emmanuel's land.

O Christ, he is the fountain,
The deep sweet well of love!
The streams on earth I've tasted
More deep I'll drink above:
There to an ocean fullness
His mercy doth expand,
And glory, glory dwelleth
In Emmanuel's land.

The bride eyes not her garment,
But her dear bridegroom's face;
I will not gaze at glory,
But on my King of grace;
Not at the crown he gifteth,

117

But on his pierced hand:
The Lamb is all the glory
Of Emmanuel's land.[4]

People often express a variety of reasons for wanting to go to heaven, not least of which is to avoid hell. But other reasons include the hope of being reunited with loved ones who have passed into glory, the longing to be rid of suffering, even the desire to live in a pleasant and beautiful place where the streets are paved with gold and where there will be no more tears or death. There is nothing wrong with these desires. They are all biblical. But the Christian longs for heaven first and foremost because Christ is there. He desires to be in the glorious presence of his Lord and Savior, enjoying uninterrupted communion with Christ. He knows only that can truly satisfy.

For the contented Christian, life is Christ, and death is infinitely more of the same.

But we also see in Philippians 1 how these heavenly values lead Paul to much earthly good. He wants what Christ wants, and so he willingly gives himself for others. The continuation of his life will be for the Philippians' "progress and joy in the faith" (v. 25). Paul follows the example of Christ who "made himself nothing, taking the form of a servant" (Phil. 2:7). The desire for Christ leads to being stamped with Christ's character.

The heavenly-minded Christian is God's gift to his church. He longs for Christ because he presently has intimate communion with Christ. And these go together. The contented Christian does not long for heaven just to escape life on earth. He longs for heaven because he already knows the sweetness of communion with Christ on earth. Heaven is already in his soul, bringing peace and contentment.

But the one who longs for Christ is also an instrument of Christ to serve others. His union with Christ transforms him and makes him like Christ. So he lives to serve, following Christ's example. And this gives the Christian contentment.

3. Contentment comes by recognizing the glorious things laid up in heaven.

The thought of the glory of heaven keeps the Christian going—and content—during times of difficulty and hardship. Paul says in Romans 8:18, "For I consider that the sufferings of this present time are not worth comparing with the glory that is to be revealed to us." This is not escapist fantasy. The Christian recognizes that this life is full of suffering. But the reality of heaven means that, for the believer, suffering is not endless or meaningless.

Paul goes on in Romans 8 to say,

> But we ourselves, who have the firstfruits of the Spirit, groan inwardly as we wait eagerly for adoption as sons, the redemption of our bodies. For in this hope we were saved. Now hope that is seen is not hope. For who hopes for what he sees? But if we hope for what we do not see, we wait for it with patience. (vv. 23–25)

The believer has hope because of the finished work of Christ and the promises of God that glorious things await him after physical death. And so he waits eagerly, patiently, confidently for these things to come.

Paul expresses a similar idea in 2 Corinthians:

So we do not lose heart. Though our outer nature is wasting away, our inner nature is being renewed day by day. For this light momentary affliction is preparing for us an eternal weight of glory beyond all comparison, as we look not to the things that are seen but to the things that are unseen. For the things that are seen are transient, but the things that are unseen are eternal. For we know that if the tent that is our earthly home is destroyed, we have a building from God, a house not made with hands, eternal in the heavens. For in this tent we groan, longing to put on our heavenly dwelling, if indeed by putting it on we may not be found naked. For while we are still in this tent, we groan, being burdened—not that we would be unclothed, but that we would be further clothed, so that what is mortal may be swallowed up by life. He who has prepared us for this very thing is God, who has given us the Spirit as a guarantee. So we are always of good courage. We know that while we are at home in the body we are away from the Lord, for we walk by faith, not by sight. Yes, we are of good courage, and we would rather be away from the body and at home with the Lord. So whether we are at home or away, we make it our aim to please him. (4:16–5:9)

This passage contains themes that are similar to what we have already seen. We see here, for instance, the desire to depart this life, expressed as "longing to put on our heavenly dwelling." We also see the earlier theme of seeking to live for Christ—"we make it our aim to please him."

But what stands out the most is the contrast between present struggles and heavenly glory. This world consists of "momentary affliction" and the experience of groaning (the same word is used here as in Romans 8:23). At the same time, Paul holds out for the Christian the confident assurance of what is to come. Beyond life in this world the believer looks forward to "an eternal weight of glory beyond all comparison." This thought keeps him steady; it keeps him going; it gives him peace and contentment.

In his book about Cambodia, *Killing Fields, Living Fields*, Don Cormack tells the story of a Christian teacher named Haim during the time when the Khmer Rouge came to power.

Haim knew that the youthful black-clad Khmer Rouge soldiers now heading across the field were coming this time for him. . . .

Leaning weakly against his hoe for support—itself ironically the primary instrument of execution—he watched their easy, menacing, unhurried pace. . . . Haim was determined that when his turn came, he would die with dignity and without complaint. Since "Liberation" on April 17, 1975, what Cambodian had not considered this day? . . .

Haim's entire family was rounded up that afternoon. They were "the old dandruff," "bad blood," "enemies of the revolution,'" "CIA agents." They were Christians.

The family spent a sleepless night comforting one another and praying for each other as they lay bound together in the dewy grass beneath a stand of friendly trees. Next morning the teenage soldiers returned and led them . . . to their place of execution . . . the "killing fields."

Curious villagers foraging in the bush nearby lingered, half hidden, watching the familiar routine as the family were ordered to dig a large grave for themselves. Then, consenting to Haim's request for a moment to prepare themselves for death, father, mother and children, hands linked, knelt together around the gaping pit. With loud cries to God, Haim began exhorting both the Khmer Rouge and all those looking on from afar to repent and believe the gospel.

Then, in panic, one of Haim's young sons leapt to his feet, bolted into the surrounding bush and disappeared. Haim jumped up and with amazing coolness and authority prevailed upon the Khmer Rouge not to pursue the lad, but allow him to call the boy back. The knots of onlookers, peering around trees, the Khmer Rouge, and the stunned family still kneeling at the graveside, looked on in awe as Haim began calling his son, pleading with him to return and die together with his family.

"What comparison, my son," he called out, "Stealing a few more days of life in the wilderness, a fugitive, wretched and alone, to joining your family here momentarily around this grave, but soon around the throne of God, free forever in Paradise?" After a few tense moments, the bushes parted, and the lad, weeping, walked slowly back to his place with the kneeling family. "Now we are ready to go," Haim told the Khmer Rouge.

By this time there was not a soldier standing there who had the heart to raise his hoe to deliver the death blow on the backs of these noble heads. Ultimately this had to be done by the Khmer Rouge commune chief, who had not witnessed these things. But few of those watching doubted that as each of these Christians' bodies toppled silently into the earthen pit which the victims themselves had prepared, their souls soared heavenward to a place prepared by the Lord.[5]

During times of severe testing, the thought of the glories of heaven, of being around the throne of God, gives the Christian security, confidence, and peace. When the end is secure, the

Christian can face life's greatest trials knowing that God is in control and that his life is hidden with God in Christ. In fact, his present communion with Christ is a foretaste of heavenly glory. The experience of heaven now fills his soul with delight and keeps him longing for more.

Those whose eyes are on this world pursue a peace they can never attain. This world does not satisfy. It amounts to a chasing after the wind. Of course, if this world is all there is, there is no alternative but to find peace in what it offers. But sadly it never comes.

The Christian, on the other hand, looks not to the things that are seen but to the things that are unseen. He fixes his eyes on heaven, recognizing that the afflictions of this life are merely preparing him for "an eternal weight of glory beyond all comparison." He longs for heaven. And his longing means contentment on earth.

Discussion Questions

1. Can you think of times in your life when the thought of heaven has given you peace and contentment? How can we foster a heavenly-mindedness in our lives?

2. Is it difficult to understand yourself as a citizen of heaven? Why or why not? How does being a citizen of heaven make us more useful on earth?

3. How does the believer's current relationship with Christ cause him to want to depart and be with Christ? Do you see this as a good desire? How does this desire lead to godliness and contentment?

CHAPTER 8

Finding Contentment in the Enjoyment of God

✠

THE CHRISTIAN FINDS contentment in longing for heaven. But heaven is already in the soul of a godly Christian. This, too, brings contentment.

The joy of heaven is full and unhindered knowledge of God. It is seeing our Lord face to face, communing with him intimately. It is being in his presence, worshipping him, delighting in him. It is knowing his comfort and security—no night, no need for the gates of the heavenly city to be shut (Rev. 21:25), no fear.

By faith, the Christian experiences each of these joys now. He is in relationship with God through Christ. He has fellowship and communion with God. He knows him personally, intimately. He has the joy of worship and delight in the presence of God. He has the comfort and security that God has betrothed him to himself forever, that no one can snatch him out of God's hand.

The Christian finds contentment in joyful fellowship with God now.

Two themes dominate Paul's letter to the Philippians. They are the believer's joy and his union with Christ. These themes are inextricably woven together. *Union with Christ* is simply another way of saying that the believer has a relationship with Christ. And this relationship is the fountain from which springs the overflow of joy in the believer's heart.

Man is a social being. He is made to be in relationship with others. This is part of being created in the image of God. The Bible teaches that the one God exists in three persons, Father, Son, and Holy Spirit, who live together in eternal fellowship. So too we were made to live in communion with others. But in particular we were made to live in fellowship and communion with God himself. When this is missing from our lives, there is disorder and discontent. As Augustine put it, "Our hearts are restless until they find their rest in you."[1]

Christian satisfaction and contentment come primarily through our relationship with God in Christ.

Thus, the Pauline emphasis on the believer's union with Christ is a glorious truth. Paul expresses this union in a number of different ways in his letters, but we find it especially, pervasively, in his phrase "in Christ" (alternatively, "in him," "in the Lord," etc.). Paul uses this expression more than any other to summarize what it means to be a Christian and to live the Christian life. It is found more than 160 times in his letters.

It is not surprising, then, to find that language expressing union with Christ is prominent in Philippians. In fact, it undergirds Paul's entire discussion in the letter. Paul begins by addressing "all the saints in Christ Jesus who are at Philippi" (1:1). He declares that his imprisonment is "in Christ" (1:13 KJV). The Philippians' boast abounds "in Christ Jesus" (1:26; cf. 3:3); they have "encouragement in Christ" (2:1); and Paul himself has hope (2:19) and confidence (2:24) "in the Lord." Paul also speaks of knowing Christ (3:8, 10), gaining Christ (3:8), being found "in him" (3:9), and sharing in his sufferings and death, as well as in the power of his resurrection (3:10).

Christ Jesus has taken hold of Paul and made Paul his own (3:12). Paul in turn presses on toward the goal to win the prize of the upward call of God "in Christ Jesus" (3:14). Believers stand firm "in the Lord" (4:1) and are to agree "in the Lord" (4:2). The peace of God guards the hearts and minds of believers "in Christ Jesus" (4:7), and the riches of God's glory are found "in Christ Jesus" (4:19).

It should come as no surprise, then, to hear Paul exhort the Philippians to "rejoice in the Lord" (3:1; 4:4; cf. 4:10). Not only is union with Christ an essential part of the Christian life—the believer's union with Christ is the source of his joy and contentment.

Now it is important to understand that the believer's union with Christ has different senses in the New Testament. There are, in other words, different ways in which the believer is united with Christ. The idea of spiritual union, expressed most explicitly in Paul's language of "Christ in" the believer (e.g., Gal. 2:20; Col. 1:27), is only one aspect of union with Christ.

We can understand this if we consider the variety of ways that we speak today of being united or being in relationship with someone. We speak of the union or merger of companies in some kind of business arrangement. Similarly, it is common for individuals to enter into a business partnership. But this is quite different from the marriage relationship and the union that exists between husband and wife. The latter is deeper, more intimate, and involves a legal, physical, and spiritual union.

When we examine the notion of union with Christ in the New Testament, two different, though inextricably interrelated forms of this union predominate. One is what we can call a covenantal or representative union. The second is an existential or spiritual union. Each of these is a source of inexpressible contentment.

1. The believer finds contentment in the covenant of grace.

Believers are first of all united with Christ in a covenantal relationship. Christ is our covenant head and representative, the mediator and "surety" (Heb. 7:22 KJV; ESV reads "guarantor") of the covenant. All of the blessings and promises of the covenant are because of Christ. They come to us because we are united with him in this covenantal union.

Paul makes a contrast in his writings between being "in Adam" and "in Christ" (1 Cor. 15:22). "In Adam" all die. But "in Christ" believers have life. The issue here is clearly not that of mystical or spiritual union. Rather, it is a matter of whether we belong to Adam or to Christ as our corporate head and representative. This is why Paul can say believers have died with Christ (Rom. 6:8) and have been raised with him (Col. 3:1). Because Christ is our corporate head and representative, what happened to Christ has also happened to us.

The good news in all of this is that Christ has done it all. Our standing with God depends on what Christ has done, not on what we do. All of the promises of God's covenant with his people will surely come to pass, because they are not based on the imperfect and unfaithful efforts of man. The promises of God are Yes and Amen "in Christ" (cf. 2 Cor. 1:19–21). In fact, this foundational covenantal union stretches back into eternity. God chose us "in [Christ] before the foundation of the world" (Eph. 1:4). The believer's covenantal union with Christ is unshakable and unbreakable.

It is against this backdrop that Paul writes of his desire to "be found in him, not having a righteousness of my own that comes from the law, but that which comes through faith in Christ, the righteousness from God that depends on faith" (Phil. 3:9). Paul recognizes that his standing with God does not depend on his own efforts or his own righteousness (cf. Phil. 3:4–7). Rather, his righteousness comes through union with Christ and is a gift from God. In Romans 5 Paul makes it clear that God's "gift of righteousness" is the obedience of Christ (vv. 15–19).

In other words, because the believer is united with Christ, Christ's righteousness becomes his righteousness. This righteousness is not imparted to the believer in the sense that he becomes personally sinless as Christ was sinless. Rather, Christ's righteousness is imputed to the believer; it is credited to his account. In terms of standing with God, when God looks at the believer, he sees the believer clothed in Christ's righteousness, and so in right relationship with himself.

This should be a source of great joy for those who trust in Christ. For those who know this truth and meditate upon it, it brings peace and contentment when we realize that our ultimate standing with God does not depend on our works or our efforts. Rather, it is because of Christ's finished work, and it comes to the believer through faith—that is, by trusting in what Christ has done, receiving the gift that God offers, and resting in Christ alone.

Burroughs speaks of getting contentment from the covenant of grace. When believers know that they are in an unbreakable and unshakable relationship with God, it gives them a humble, quiet confidence and contentment. When David was coming to the end of his life, he declared, "For does not my house stand so with God? For he has made with me an everlasting covenant, ordered in all things and secure. For will he not cause to prosper all my help and my desire?" (2 Sam. 23:5). David rested secure in God's eternal covenant, even though the circumstances in his life were not smooth and easy, and trouble would beset his house after his death as well. Still, he took refuge in God's covenant with him.

One writer refers to a covenant as a "bond-in-blood, sovereignly administered."[2] Because God has established an everlasting bond with his people through the life, death, resurrection, and ascension of Christ, Christians can stand firm in the midst of turmoil and trouble, knowing that their relationship with God is secure.

One of the tragedies of modern life is that we have lost a sense of marriage as a covenant, a solemn bond that one enters into that can be broken only on pain of death. Marriage is not easy, and the difficulties of marriage can only be endured and overcome when a couple believes in "till death do us part." Without this knowledge, marriage is insecure and on shaky ground.

But God's covenant is always secure, always firm. And the believer finds contentment in that.

Genesis 15 is a passage of Scripture that is strange to modern readers of the Bible. In this passage God tells Abraham (at that time called Abram) to bring to him a variety of animals. Abraham does so. But Abraham also cuts them in half and lays each half on the ground opposite the other half. God then brings a deep sleep on Abraham and passes between the pieces of the animals in the form of a smoking pot and flaming torch.

This sounds like a grotesque, bloody scene. Is there any significance to it? Indeed there is, when we understand it in light of the ancient custom of how people entered into a covenant with one another.

The ceremony described in Genesis 15 was the basic ceremony by which men entered into a binding covenant with each other. They would cut animals in two, and then both parties would walk between the pieces. The cutting of the animals is actually reflected in the consistent Old Testament language for entering into a covenant—literally in the Hebrew, "cutting a covenant." The point of walking between the pieces is to say, "May what has happened to these animals happen to me if I don't keep this binding covenantal agreement." A covenant was broken on pain of death.

The glorious message of Genesis 15 was that God was saying that if the covenant was not kept, then he himself would be cut off for his people. This was a foreshadowing of the cross, in which Christ, the Son of God, was put to death for the sins of his people under the covenant of grace.

In God's covenant of grace, a great exchange has taken place. Christ has taken our sin and has borne the wrath of God that we deserved for our sin. Our sins are forgiven. There is no curse, no condemnation.

But that's not all. Those who trust in Christ, who are united to him by faith, also gain his righteousness. All must have a righteousness to claim and to present to God. There is no salvation without it. Some seek to present their own good works. But our works can never meet God's perfect standard. We are saved only by the righteousness of Christ being given to us.

This great exchange under the covenant of grace is a great source of peace and rest for the Christian. The reason is that it tells us salvation is not based on what we do or even on how we feel. We are saved because of Christ's finished work on our behalf. Christians find contentment in the truth of God's covenant.

But we also find contentment in the promises of the covenant. In the ancient world, including the Bible, promises were a key component of covenants. One party would promise to do certain things, and the other party would promise to respond in kind. If we look again at Genesis 15, we see that the covenant ceremony is framed by God's promises to Abraham.

Before Abraham divides the animals, God tells him that his descendants will be as the stars of heaven. Afterward God promises Abraham that God will give him land:

> On that day the LORD made a covenant with Abram, saying, "To your offspring I give this land, from the river of Egypt to the great river, the river Euphrates, the land of the Kenites, the Kenizzites, the Kadmonites, the Hittites, the Perizzites, the Rephaim, the Amorites, the Canaanites, the Girgashites and the Jebusites." (Gen. 15:18–21)

God here confirms these promises and ensures that he will make good on his word by passing between the parts of the animals.

In the same way, the death of Christ gives the Christian assurance that the promises of God will come to fruition. As Paul puts it, "For all the promises of God find their Yes in [Christ]" (2 Cor. 1:20).

What are some of these promises? It is good to recall them, to reflect on them, and to rest assured in the promises of God to his people. Puritan pastor Samuel Clarke has done a great service to the church in compiling a long list of the promises that God has made to his people. Clarke has divided them into a number of categories that apply to a variety of situations that we face in life. I do not intend to reproduce all of those promises here. I simply point the reader to Clarke's work (*Precious Bible Promises*; also known as *Clarke's Scripture Promises*) and encourage you to meditate on these precious promises of God. For our purposes, we'll reflect on a few key promises that God has made to his people.

First, God promises never to leave or forsake his children. This promise was first given to Joshua as an encouragement to carry out the work that God had called him to do (Josh. 1:5). He could be strong and courageous because God would always be with him. But this promise is repeated in various ways throughout the Bible and is given to all of God's people. We find it most explicitly in Hebrews 13:5, in the context of contentment: "Keep your life free from love of money, and be content with what you have, for he has said, 'I will never leave you nor forsake you.'" The believer is to rest content in God's provision because God will not forsake him. He will supply what the Christian needs.

A second "precious promise" of God's covenant is that "he who began a good work in you will bring it to completion at the day of Jesus Christ" (Phil. 1:6). God will carry on the work that he is doing in and among his people. Unlike many human beings who begin a job and never finish, God will always complete the work that he has started. This is especially encouraging in our pursuit of sanctification. When we see the weight of our sin or fall under the pressures of temptation, we can find peace in knowing that God will continue his transforming work in our lives. He is now conforming us to the image of Christ and will not cease until that process is consummated (Rom. 8:29–30).

Third, God has promised that "for those who love God all things work together for good, for those who are called according to his purpose" (Rom. 8:28). This statement in Romans 8 comes in the context of persecution and suffering (cf. 8:18, 35–36). In times of difficulty, the Christian finds contentment in knowing that his hardship is purposeful and productive. God is working for our good and for his glory. We need not, we must not despair.

Fourth, in the same glorious chapter God also promises that he will not only sustain us, but that he will graciously give us all things: "He who did not spare his own Son but gave him up for us all, how will he not also with him graciously give us all things?" (v. 32). The Christian is assured of an abundance of blessings at God's right hand. God is not a stingy giver. The delight and the joy of the Christian will overflow in Christ.

We could continue along these lines forever, reflecting on God's promises of security ("no one will snatch them out of my hand," John 10:28), strength ("you will receive power," Acts 1:8), service ("you will be my witnesses," Acts 1:8), and provision (Matt. 6:25–34). But the greatest of God's covenant promises is simply the promise of his presence.

2. The Christian finds contentment in being united to the God of the covenant.

God's relationship with his people is not a detached, sterile, legal relationship of give and take. Rather, in the covenant of grace God comes to his people. The heart of God's covenant of grace is the twofold promise, "I will be your God, and you will be my people," or simply stated, "I will be with you." In the covenant of grace, God takes a people to himself to be his special possession. He promises to dwell in their midst.

But there is more. God promises not only to be with them but also to be in them. God takes up residence in the heart of each of his people. Jesus tells his disciples,

I will ask the Father, and he will give you another Helper, to be with you forever, even the Spirit of truth, whom the world

135

cannot receive, because it neither sees him nor knows him.
You know him, for he dwells with you and will be in you.
(John 14:16–17)

Notice the two aspects of the Spirit's dwelling—"with you"
and "in you." The Spirit is not only present in the midst of his
people, he is present within them. Jesus goes on to say that
the indwelling Spirit is no less than his own presence: "In that
day you will know that I am in my Father, and you in me, and
I in you" (John 14:20).

The believer has a vital spiritual union with Jesus Christ.
In the Philippians 3 passage quoted earlier, Paul moves
quickly from the believer's status in Christ because of
imputed righteousness ("and be found in him, not having a
righteousness of my own that comes from the law, but that
which comes through faith in Christ, the righteousness from
God that depends on faith," 3:9) to the believer's intimate
relationship with Christ—"that I may know him and the
power of his resurrection, and may share his sufferings,
becoming like him in his death" (3:10). Paul desires to
know Christ in every aspect of his life and being, from the
heights of resurrection power to the depths of sacrificial
suffering. The experience of the fullness of Christ's life is
life itself and is the fount of joy, peace, and contentment
for the believer.

To return to the marriage analogy used earlier, in one
sense my marriage is a legal covenant. I am legally, objec-
tively, externally united to my wife in the eyes of God and
the state. But if my relationship to my wife is only legal,
objective, external, then I am missing the fullness of joy

that marriage offers. The fact is, I delight in my wife. I find joy in talking with her, laughing with her, crying with her. Our times of physical intimacy are among life's greatest pleasures. In an earthly sense, she satisfies me in every way.

But even the satisfaction of my wife can never truly satisfy the deepest longings of my soul. In fact, I sin against my wife if I attempt to find my deepest satisfaction in her. Only an Infinite Person can truly satisfy us.

This is a mystery to a world that seeks satisfaction in finite people and things. Ours is a world that constantly seeks greater fulfillment. When a marriage ceases to be personally fulfilling, we move on in search of another. When a job is no longer exciting, we look for a new one, or we seek diversions through the media and entertainment.

In fact, it is the lack of fulfillment that has led to our booming entertainment culture. Jesus told his disciples, "You are the salt of the earth" (Matt. 5:13). Salt gives flavor. Jesus is implicitly saying that without the church and its message of salvation in Christ, the world has no flavor. Life in the world is meaningless, without purpose.

Marie Antoinette once famously exclaimed, "Nothing tastes!" That appears to be the common sentiment in our world today. A common statement that I hear from my kids is, "I'm bored." Life is boring to many today. Entertainment fills the boredom of life.

But filling does not equal fulfilling. Entertainment can fill our meaningless existence, but it never gives fulfillment, joy, contentment. Only an intimate relationship with God through Jesus Christ can do that. And the Christian can and must continually go to the source of his joy, strength, peace, and contentment.

When I travel, I am typically away from my wife for less than half a day before I long to get back to her. In an even greater way, the Christian should long to return to the presence of Christ. Of course, in one sense, because Christ lives in us, he is always with us. But in another sense the believer needs times of intimate communion with Christ, spending time in prayer, Bible reading, praise, and meditation on the Word of God. It is especially in those times of sweet fellowship that the Christian feels the presence of Christ and the joy of union with him.

In the next chapter we will see that our union with Christ also extends to Christ's character being formed in us and that contentment also comes in following Christ's example of sacrificial service. But for now it is sufficient to reflect on the often neglected need for intimate communion with the Living Lord.

The church has long advocated the spiritual disciplines of prayer and meditation as being vital not only to the *power* of the Christian life but also to the *peace* of the Christian life. As Paul concludes Philippians, he exhorts his readers to practice these very things. First, Paul exhorts them not to "be anxious about anything, but in everything by prayer and supplication with thanksgiving let your requests be made known to God" (Phil. 4:6). The Christian is to pray at all times, in all circumstances, but especially in times of anxiety. When we pray, the peace of God replaces our anxious, unsettled spirit: "And the peace of God, which surpasses all understanding, will guard your hearts and your minds in Christ Jesus" (4:7).

Second, Paul goes on to exhort the Philippians to "think about," or meditate on, those things that are true, honorable, just, pure, lovely, commendable, excellent, and worthy of praise (4:8). In other words, the Christian is to meditate on Christ, his attributes, and his revelation. Once again this is followed by the promise of peace (4:9). These commands to pray and meditate, furthermore, are set in the context of rejoicing (4:4) and contentment (4:11–13). The believer finds contentment not just because he practices certain disciplines, but rather because in these disciplines he has intimate communion with Jesus Christ.

Scripture commands us to "taste and see that the LORD is good" (Ps. 34:8). It promises us that at "[his] right hand are pleasures forevermore" (Ps. 16:11). The believer's attitude is to be that of the psalmist who prayed, "As a deer pants for flowing streams, so pants my soul for you, O God" (Ps. 42:1). The pleasures of this world do not satisfy. Only God can satisfy.

The joy, the desire, the delight of the Christian is found in God alone. In fact, sometimes God takes away our earthly pleasures so that we can find greater delight in him. The water pressure in our home is not the best. It is fine if water is running in only one place. But if two people are taking showers, it is weak. If a shower is running, someone's doing dishes, and someone else is running water in the sink, the water comes out as a trickle. To get a good shower, I have to make sure water is not running from any other source.

In the same way, God sometimes turns off the other sources of our pleasure so that we might learn to find all of our delight in him. He must be our desire. He is our all in all. And only when we delight in him alone do we find true contentment.

As Charles Simeon lay dying, someone asked him, "What are you thinking now?" Simeon replied, "I don't think now. I am enjoying."[3]

Simeon's life was devoted to fellowship with God in Christ. His approaching death meant for him full, unhindered communion with his Lord. A life of the enjoyment of God would lead to greater joy in the life to come. So instead of fear and anxiety Simeon's final days were marked by enjoyment. Indeed, only as our lives are marked by communion with God can we live and die with contentment.

Burroughs writes, "No soul shall ever come to heaven, but the soul which has heaven come to it first." The Christian experiences a foretaste of glory as he lives in vital union and communion with God in Christ. This is the root of our contentment.

Discussion Questions

1. Make a list of the things that give you the most joy and satisfaction in life. Now go back and number the list, with number one being the thing that gives you the most joy. Be honest. Is your worship of and fellowship with God at the top of that list? Are there any activities that you need to cut out of your life so God can be your all in all?

2. Would you say your life is characterized by joyful, vital fellowship with Christ? Give an honest assessment of your prayer life. Do you meditate on God and his Word?

3. How can you find contentment in God's covenant of grace?

4. List some of the precious promises of God that bring you the most peace. What are some ways you can be more intentional in meditating on these promises?

CHAPTER 9

The Contentment of Being Conformed to the Image of Christ

✠

OUR HOME IS FILLED with trophies that our six kids have received simply for participating in a sport. I have always thought this to be strange. When I was growing up, those who participated were always recognized. But trophies were reserved for those who excelled—Most Valuable Player, Best Offensive Player, Coach's Award, etc. It makes me feel especially strange, if not downright irritated, when I am asked to pay extra money to buy the trophy for participation that I don't think my child should be given in the first place!

This is the nature of our world today, at least in the United States. Self-esteem has become one of our most cherished values. Our educational system is geared toward creating self-esteem in children. Individual achievement and recognition of excellence are not as important as making sure that everyone feels good about themselves. If we give trophies to some and not to others, someone's feelings might be hurt. It might affect their self-esteem. Or so the conventional wisdom goes.

Within this context, the world says that the way to happiness is to "be yourself." It exhorts us that we need to like ourselves, to have self-esteem. Sometimes the Bible is even twisted to reflect this. Scripture teaches us to "love your neighbor as yourself." This is often interpreted today as meaning that we must love ourselves first before we can love our neighbor. But the reality is that we do love ourselves in the sense that we look out for our own best interests. In the same way, we are to look out for the interests of others.

In contrast to today's emphasis on self-esteem, the biblical message is that contentment only comes from *not* being ourselves. That is, we find peace and joy from being conformed to the image of Christ.

The Bible is clear that every human being has dignity because he or she has been created in the image of God. But sin has marred that image. The goal, indeed the end result for the believer, is conformity to Christ, who is himself described in Scripture (drawing on creation language) as the "image" of God. In other words, Christianity is about restoring human beings to the state that God originally intended for them.

In a sense, then, we can say that Christianity is about *becoming* ourselves, not *being* ourselves. Simply being ourselves in our sin and depravity leads to death and despair. There is no joy in that. The believer has hope only as he sees the character of Christ being formed in him.

The Bible uses the term *glorification* (or, *being glorified*) to refer to the final state of believers. In that state, there is no more sin, no more death and decay. The believer is completely and forever conformed to the image of Christ, having a radiance and perfect righteousness like his. John writes, "Beloved, we are God's children now, and what we will be has not yet appeared; but we know that when he appears we shall be like him, because we shall see him as he is" (1 John 3:2). At Christ's second coming, all of God's children will be transformed and will become like him.

The apostle Paul puts it this way:

> For those whom he foreknew he also predestined to be conformed to the image of his Son, in order that he might be the firstborn among many brothers. And those whom he predestined he also called, and those whom he called he also justified, and those whom he justified he also glorified. (Rom. 8:29–30)

The first line of verse 29 is parallel to verse 30, clearly linked by the word "predestined." Being "predestined to be conformed to the image of" Christ means being predestined to be "glorified." Glorification is still future, though Paul here puts it in the past tense because of its certainty. But glorification means transformation and conformation to the image of Christ.

At the same time, the New Testament describes the believer's conformity to the image of Christ as an ongoing process that is now under way. To describe this, we use a different term— namely, sanctification. Sanctification means the process of being made holy, which means to be made more like Christ.

The apostle Paul says, "And we all, with unveiled face, beholding the glory of the Lord, are being transformed into the same image from one degree of glory to another" (2 Cor. 3:18). As the believer has fellowship and communion with Christ (see chapter 8), "beholding the glory of Lord," he is progressively transformed into his image. The final phrase above literally reads "from glory to glory." Final, full glorification awaits Christ's return. But conformity to his image is now under way. Indeed, without this process there is no godly contentment.

Before returning to Philippians to see how these truths are present there, I want to return to the discussion of union with Christ from chapter 8. Paul makes clear that when we are united to Christ we are in the process of being conformed to his image.

The most striking language that Paul uses to refer to the believer's union with Christ is his affirmation of "Christ in" the believer (Gal. 2:20; Col. 1:27; Rom. 8:10; 2 Cor. 13:5). "Christ in" us means that we have a vital spiritual union with Christ. But in context each of these references also points to Christ's character being formed in us. Christ dwells in every believer. And because of this a radical change takes place. By his presence I become conformed to his image.

Colossians 1:27 epitomizes Paul's "Christ in" passages: "To them God chose to make known how great among the Gentiles are the riches of the glory of this mystery, which is Christ in you, the hope of glory." The believer's relationship with Christ now ("Christ in you") gives assurance of the glorious inheritance to come ("the hope of glory"). This is a great source of contentment. Yet it is a source of contentment only as the believer seeks to grow and build on his relationship with Christ.

As Paul battles false teaching in Colossae (see Col. 2:8–23), one of his goals is to see the Colossians grow to maturity. Thus, he follows his "Christ in you" statement with the following: "Him we proclaim, warning everyone and teaching everyone with all wisdom, that we may present everyone mature in Christ" (Colossians 1:28). This maturity includes the growth of Christlike character, and so in Colossians 3 Paul returns to his "Christ in" language:

> Do not lie to one another, seeing that you have put off the old self with its practices and have put on the new self, which is being renewed in knowledge after the image of its creator. Here there is not Greek and Jew, circumcised and uncircumcised, barbarian, Scythian, slave, free; but Christ is all, and in all. (vv. 9–11)

"Christ . . . in all" means the putting off of the old self and putting on "the new self, which is being renewed in knowledge after the image of its creator." The "creator" here is clearly Christ (cf. 1:16). Thus, to have Christ in you means to be made new after Christ's image.

Paul spells this out in practical terms in the verses that follow (3:12–17). Believers are to "put on" the characteristics of Christ, especially "compassionate hearts, kindness, humility, meekness, and patience" (v. 12). They are to forgive each other "as the Lord has forgiven you" (v. 13). They are to show Christlike love to one another (v. 14). And they are to "let the peace of Christ rule in [their] hearts" (v. 15).

The development of Christlike character is both a fact— "you . . . have put on the new self" (3:9–10)—and a responsibility—"put on then" (3:12). But the point is clear: The vital, spiritual union that the believer has with Christ means a transformation and conformation to Christ's image.

Let's return now to Philippians, the letter that has been the focus of this study. "Joy" marks almost every paragraph of the letter. But "be joyful" is not the main message that Paul wants to communicate. At the heart of the letter is a great passage about Christ:

> Have this mind among yourselves, which is yours in Christ Jesus, who, though he was in the form of God, did not count equality with God a thing to be grasped, but made himself nothing, taking the form of a servant, being born in the likeness of men. And being found in human form, he humbled himself by becoming obedient to the point of death, even death on a cross. Therefore God has highly exalted him and bestowed on him the name that is above every name, so that at the name of Jesus every knee should bow, in heaven and on earth and under the earth, and every tongue confess that Jesus Christ is Lord, to the glory of God the Father. (2:5–11)

This passage beautifully depicts the heart of the gospel. Christ, though being God, humbled himself by taking to himself a human nature and submitting to death on a cross. He exposed himself to suffering and dishonor in contrast to the worship and glory that he had always known. He came as a servant, being concerned not primarily about his own rights but about the good of others.

But notice how this passage begins. Believers are to have the mind of Christ. They are to think as he thought, to walk as he walked.

As many commentators have pointed out, the main theme of Philippians is expressed two verses prior to the passage quoted above: "in humility count others more significant than yourselves" (Phil. 2:3). Philippians, Paul's letter of joy, is also a letter about humble service on behalf of others. In fact, these two themes go together. Without self-abasement and selfless service for others the Christian life is joyless.

Contentment comes in considering others above ourselves and giving ourselves to serve them.

A careful reading of Philippians indicates that this is the key theme of the letter. We see this from the opening verse. In 1:1 Paul addresses not only "all the saints" in Philippi but also the "overseers and deacons." This beginning is unique among Paul's letters. He also begins by referring to himself not as an apostle, as he does in nine of his thirteen letters, but as a "servant." In other words, Paul begins by honoring the leaders of the church in Philippi. He gives an example of considering others above himself.

As we read on, we find that this is the very heartbeat of the letter. Later in chapter 1, Paul indicates that his desire is to depart and be with Christ (1:23). His life is Christ, so death is gain (1:21) because it means more of Christ. But he submits his desires to the good of the Philippians and their growth in grace:

> But to remain in the flesh is more necessary on your account.
> Convinced of this, I know that I will remain and continue with
> you all, for your progress and joy in the faith. (1:24–25)

Paul is more concerned about humble service to others for their spiritual good than he is about personal gratification.

Skipping over the beginning of chapter 2 and the great Christological passage, we see later in the chapter two examples of selfless, Christlike service. Paul tells of his desire

149

to send Timothy to visit the Philippians. Timothy, unlike others who seek their own interests (2:21), is "genuinely concerned" for the welfare of the Philippians, and ultimately for the interests of Christ (2:20–21). Likewise, Epaphroditus is an example of one who poured himself out, even coming close to death, for the sake of Christ and his church (2:25–30).

At the heart of Paul's discussion, then, he presents Christ as the supreme example of one who did not cling to his own rights, who abased himself, and who gave himself for others. The point is clear: Believers are to live in humble service, considering others above themselves, pouring themselves out for others. This is the path to the joy and contentment that are so critical to Paul's discussion in Philippians.

My sister and brother-in-law have a cross-stitch up in their home that reads, "Happy is the heart that beats for others." Joy and contentment come not in self-esteem, in self-fulfillment, in living for self. Rather, they come in living for others. Christ-esteem and other-esteem are what matter.

Charles Spurgeon once said,

> O, there is nothing that can so advantage you, nothing can so prosper you, so assist you, so make you walk towards heaven rapidly, so keep your heads upwards toward the sky, and your eyes radiant with glory, like the imitation of Jesus Christ. It is when, by the power of the Holy Spirit, you are enabled to walk with Jesus in his very footsteps, and tread in his ways, you are most happy and you are most known to be sons and daughters of God. For your sake, Christ, I say, be like Christ. To draw him nearer to me, and myself nearer to him, is the innermost longing of my soul.[1]

To be like Christ, walking in love just as he loved us and gave himself up for us (Eph. 5:1–2)—that is the source of joy in the Christian life.

Lying behind Paul's concern for self-giving service in his letter to the Philippians appears to be, at least in part, a squabble between two women who had been his coworkers, Euodia and Syntyche (4:2–3). In other words, he is concerned for unity in the body of Christ. Humble service and considering others above ourselves are essential to unity.

From a biblical perspective, peace with God, peace with others, and peace within ourselves are all tied together.[2] This is true for a number of reasons. First, the Bible commands us to love and be at peace with one another. Paul writes, "If possible, so far as it depends on you, live peaceably with all" (Rom. 12:18). There can be no internal peace for the one who does not keep the commands of God.

Second, the Holy Spirit establishes a unity with other believers. Paul tells the Ephesians to be "eager to maintain the unity of the Spirit in the bond of peace" (Eph. 4:3). He does not say to "create" the unity of the Spirit. It is already a fact. The Holy Spirit within us means that our spirit is one with others who also have the Holy Spirit. But we need to maintain this unity in practice. The indwelling Spirit compels us to be united to others in whom he dwells. When this unity is lacking, the Spirit within prevents peace within. The bond of peace is fragmented.

Third, unity in the body of Christ is part of what it means to be made new in the image of God. The God of the Bible is one God in three persons. There is unity and community in the Godhead. To be made in the image of

God, therefore, means in part that we were created to live together with others in unity and community. The fall and sin fragment human relationships. When God makes each of us a new creation in Christ, those broken relationships are restored. If we are to be the people that God has remade us to be, we must live together in unity with the rest of God's new creatures.

Fourth, lack of unity affects our growth in grace. The individualism of our age has influenced the way many evangelicals think about the Christian life. For many, the Christian life and spiritual growth are simply between Jesus and me. But this is dramatically different from what the Bible teaches. Paul prays for the Ephesians,

> that Christ may dwell in your hearts through faith—that you, being rooted and grounded in love, may have strength to comprehend with all the saints what is the breadth and length and height and depth, and to know the love of Christ that surpasses knowledge, that you may be filled with all the fullness of God. (Eph. 3:17–19)

Paul clearly indicates that the Christian faith is personal—Christ dwells in the hearts of his people. But our growth in Christ—knowing the love of Christ, being filled with all the fullness of God—comes only when we are "rooted and grounded in love" and takes place "with all the saints." It is a corporate endeavor. We grow, and so experience more and more of God's peace, only in the unity and community of the body of Christ.

Humble service and unity in the body of Christ go together and are essential for the life of faith. In John's Gospel, much of Jesus' final discourse with his disciples focuses on their love, union, and communion with Christ himself and with one another (chapters 13–17). He prays to the Father "that they may be one, even as we are one" (17:11).

Significantly, these five chapters of Scripture, devoted largely to Jesus' final teachings, begin with the account of Jesus' washing his disciples' feet.

> Jesus, knowing that the Father had given all things into his hands, and that he had come from God and was going back to God, rose from supper. He laid aside his outer garments, and taking a towel, tied it around his waist. Then he poured water into a basin and began to wash the disciples' feet and to wipe them with the towel that was wrapped around him. (John 13:3–5)

He then goes on to teach them the following:

> If I then, your Lord and Teacher, have washed your feet, you also ought to wash one another's feet. For I have given you an example, that you also should do just as I have done to you. Truly, truly, I say to you, a servant is not greater than his master, nor is a messenger greater than the one who sent him. If you know these things, blessed are you if you do them. (vv. 14–17)

In this account, Jesus demonstrates the extent of his love for his disciples. He also indicates his willingness to serve them, even unto death (cf. 13:1). But his selfless service, doing the task reserved for only the lowest slave, is also to be an example for his followers. They are to serve one another as Christ has served them. In fact, those who do this are "blessed" (or "happy," as the King James Version reads; v. 17).

In his wonderful essay "No Little People, No Little Places,"[3] Francis Schaeffer reflects on the biblical theme of selfless service. He begins by considering Moses' rod. Moses' rod was simply a stick of wood, a shepherd's staff. Yet that rod became the instrument by which God performed wonders in Egypt and delivered his people from slavery.

The rod of Moses became a serpent and swallowed the serpents of the Egyptian magicians. With the rod Moses struck the Nile, and it was turned to blood. Moses stretched forth his rod, and the plagues of frogs, lice, hail, and locusts came upon the land of Egypt. And when the Israelites were trapped between the sea on one side and the Egyptian army on the other, Moses lifted up his rod, and God made a way of escape for his people.

How did an insignificant piece of wood become an instrument of great power? Exodus 4:20 gives us the answer: Moses' rod became "the rod of God" (KJV; ESV, "staff of God").

In the same way, God uses insignificant people with meager gifts to do his work in the world, sometimes in ways that affect the course of history. But, as Schaeffer puts it, "that which is *me* must become the *me* of God. Then I can become useful in God's hands. The Scripture emphasizes that much can come from little if the little is truly consecrated to God. There are no little people and no big people in the true spiritual sense, but only consecrated and unconsecrated people."[4]

Likewise, there are no little places. God wants us to be wholly committed to him in the place where God puts us. Our tendency is to want to do big works in big places. But this is the desire of the flesh, or as Schaeffer puts it, the desire of the "old, unconverted, egoist, self-centered *Me*."[5]

We are often tempted to say, "I will take the larger place because it will give me more influence for Jesus Christ." But grasping for this larger place has two problems. First, it is in the lowest place that we can more easily be quiet before the face of God. As Schaeffer says,

> Quietness and peace before God are more important than any influence a position may seem to give, for we must stay in step with God to have the power of the Holy Spirit. If by taking a bigger place our quietness with God is lost, then to that extent our fellowship with him is broken and we are living in the flesh, and the final result will not be as great, no matter how important the larger place may look in the eyes of other men or in our own eyes.[6]

Second, the attempt to lay hold of the larger place is contradictory to the biblical descriptions of greatness and of ministry. Jesus said, "But whoever would be great among you must be your servant, and whoever would be first among you must be slave of all" (Mark 10:43–44). The greatest in the Kingdom is the one who serves. But humble service in humble places is typically also where we see God's power most revealed.

Our attitude is to be that of the humble servant, who takes the lowly place and faithfully serves there. God may move us up to a larger place as he determines, but only when we are ready for it. But that is not the important thing. The important thing is "to be consecrated persons in God's place for us, at each moment."

Be content with your gifts. Be content with your place of service. But use your gifts to the glory of God.

We can summarize this chapter by saying that the key to the Christian life, and to achieving godly contentment, is dying to self. Indeed, our biggest enemy is self. We were created to glorify God and to live for him. But in our rebellion we live not for God but for self.

Jesus, then, came to save us from self. How? Precisely by giving himself. He did not cling to his own rights. He did not grasp the prerogatives of deity, but he made himself nothing. Jesus, in a sense, died to self to save us from self, so that we can die to self. Jesus' act of self-giving saves us from the sin of self-centered rebellion. But his self-giving also becomes the example for our life of dying to self and living for God.

Thus, the apostle Paul can say, "I have been crucified with Christ. It is no longer I who live, but Christ who lives in me" (Gal. 2:20). And further, "But far be it from me to boast except in the cross of our Lord Jesus Christ, by which the world has been crucified to me, and I to the world" (Gal. 6:14).

This is the consecrated life—a life lived not for self but for God. But it is also the contented life. Dead to self. Conformed to the image of Christ who gave himself for us. Free to live for God and others. This is the life of joy that the book of Philippians celebrates.

Discussion Questions

1. In what ways do you see the worldly philosophy of self-esteem and living for self present in your life? Why is it that

this worldly philosophy can never lead to the contentment that the world craves?

2. The life described in this chapter is essentially what we can call a gospel-saturated life. Why is a life of dying to self and living in humble service to God and others so closely tied to the gospel itself?

3. Have you ever thought of your own inner peace as being tied to your peace with other Christians? Are there individuals to whom you need to go and be reconciled? Make a plan to follow through on this.

4. Finding delight in God and dying to self go hand in hand. How does our delight in God lead to the denial of self, and how can the denial of self increase our delight in God?

5. Have you experienced times in your life when selfless service has led to the joy and contentment that Paul describes in Philippians? How can you make that selfless service not an occasional event but a lifestyle?

CONCLUSION

The Riches of Godliness with Contentment

✠

BLAISE PASCAL wrote, "Happiness can be found neither in ourselves nor in external things, but in God and in ourselves as united to him."[1] This is a succinct summation of biblical contentment. Human beings were created with a soul-thirst for God. Nothing but God can satisfy that thirst.

Writing to his beloved friend and coworker Timothy, Paul said,

> Now there is great gain in godliness with contentment, for we brought nothing into the world, and we cannot take anything out of the world. But if we have food and clothing, with these we will be content. (1 Tim. 6:6–8)

Godliness with contentment is great gain. This is the type of wealth that the Christian must pursue. There is a godly discontent in this pursuit. The Christian will not attain perfect holiness in this life. He longs to see the glory of God by sight, no longer simply by faith. Yet the riches of this pursuit are incomparably greater than all the vainglory of this world.

In 1 Timothy 6, Paul returns to an issue that has been prominent in the letter—false teachers. False teachers will always have a restless, discontented spirit because they fail to submit to God's authority in both doctrine and conduct. As Paul says in chapter 1, they have turned away from "a good conscience and a sincere faith" (v. 5). They are "puffed up with conceit" (6:4), rejecting God's revelation and asserting human teaching. In Scripture the arrogant is not the one who is convinced he is correct. The arrogant person is the one who asserts his reasoning and his way over against God's revealed will. True contentment is only for the humble, who submit to God's truth and God's law.

In addition to bad theology and bad ethics, the false teachers also have bad motives. They imagine "that godliness is a means of gain" (6:5). "Godliness" here means supposed godliness or the appearance of godliness. The false teachers seem to have taught a strict asceticism (4:1–5), denying themselves things that God created as good (4:4) and gave us for our enjoyment (6:17). As Paul tells the Colossians, strict teaching about food, drink, and the body has "an appearance of wisdom," even though it is of no value in restraining the sinful nature (Col. 2:23). But while teaching self-denial, these false teachers were greedy for gain. They were seeking to attract followers and patrons through their persuasion and air of superiority.

Sadly, many in the church today fall into this category. They boast of their strict life, denying themselves many creature comforts, and their spirituality, getting up early for prayer and Bible study. Others are attracted to them and admire them for their discipline. But beneath the façade of a rigorous spirituality, they are teeming with ungodly desire. You see this in the fruit of their lives—"puffed up with conceit," "an unhealthy craving for controversy," producing "constant friction" (6:4–5). The "gain" they seek may be wealth, but it could also be prestige, status, or power. In this case, the pursuit of "godliness" never leads to the quiet spirit that is true Christian contentment.

Over against this, Paul extols the "great gain" of "godliness with contentment" (6:6). 1 Timothy 6:6–10 reminds us of several biblical truths that are vital to our pursuit of contentment.

First, Paul reminds us that we are pilgrims and strangers in the world—"we brought nothing into the world, and we cannot take anything out of the world" (6:7). This is a reminder that we are just passing through. This world is not our home. We will leave this world and go to our eternal destiny. We cannot take anything with us.

When we are in a foreign land, we expect that we will be without many of the creature comforts of home. I recently spent two weeks teaching in Ukraine, living in sparse conditions quite unlike what I normally experience. I was in a very small room with a bathroom barely big enough to turn around in. My bed was uncomfortable. The food was . . . different! I often took cold showers. I encountered those whose ways and manners were quite unlike the genteel culture of the American South that I had come to know and love. I could have complained—and on occasion inwardly did so. But I simply adjusted my expectations to life in new surroundings as a stranger there.

In the same way, the Christian needs to recognize that he is a pilgrim and stranger in this world. We need to adjust our expectations and learn to live without expecting our desires to be met. We will never know contentment until we develop this mindset.

Second, Paul reminds us of the vanity of the things of the world. When he says, "we cannot take anything out of the world," he is essentially saying that the things of this world are of no ultimate spiritual value. They cannot secure our way to God. They cannot produce godliness and contentment in this life.

The Preacher declares, "Vanity of vanities! All is vanity" (Eccles. 1:2). On the one hand, all that God created is good. On the other hand, the things of this world do not satisfy our deepest longings. Human beings were created to be in relationship with God. The human soul or spirit longs for this, even when the knowledge of God is suppressed (Rom. 1:21–23). But the creature, whether as an object of affection or object of worship, can never replace the Creator.

The Rime of the Ancient Mariner laments, "Water, water everywhere, nor any drop to drink." The water of the salty sea cannot quench the thirsty man. So also, the material world that surrounds us cannot satisfy the soul's longing for the ultimate and eternal. The human being, created in the image of God, thirsts for the transcendent.

The good news is that the transcendent God is also a personal God who delights in being in relationship with his people. God invites us to taste and see that he is good (Ps. 34:8). Jesus calls the thirsty to come to him and drink (John 7:37). The one who comes to him will not hunger, the one who believes in him will never thirst (John 6:35). He tells the woman at the well, "Everyone who drinks of this [well] water will be thirsty again, but whoever drinks of the water that I will give him will never be thirsty forever. The water that I will give him will become in him a spring of water welling up to eternal life" (John 4:13–14). The psalmist says of those who take refuge under the shadow of God's wings, "They feast on the abundance of your house, and you give them drink from the river of your delights" (Ps. 36:8).

As the last paragraph indicates, the Bible speaks much of eating and drinking, especially as a metaphor for our relationship with God. The satisfaction of a good meal is a common human experience. I recently celebrated Thanksgiving with my family. For some reason, this year's meal was especially exceptional (and costly to my waistline!). Few things in life compare to the sheer pleasure of fellowship around the table and savoring good food and drink together.

One of my favorite movies is *Babette's Feast*. In this movie a woman named Babette moves into a small rural community characterized by sparse living and tense relationships. But Babette is a gourmet cook, and she decides to make a gourmet meal for all the residents. The meal begins in an awkward, uncertain, and tense fashion. The people are uncertain what they are eating, skeptical of the lavish preparations, not sure they should be there, and not happy about their dining companions. But as the meal goes on, the enjoyment increases, and the barriers begin to come down. The suspicion and tension turn to enjoyment and peace.

The Bible depicts God's people as frequently eating with one another. On several occasions Jesus attended a meal or a banquet. In fact, he evidently did that so frequently that he is called "A glutton and a drunkard, a friend of tax collectors and sinners!" (Luke 7:34). Luke describes the early Christians in this way: "day by day, attending the temple together and breaking bread in their homes, they received their food with glad and generous hearts" (Acts 2:46). First-century Judaism taught that at the end of the age there will be a great Messianic banquet. This fits with the festivals described in the Old Testament and with Zechariah's prophecy of an eschatological Feast of Tabernacles (Zech. 14:16, 18). Revelation also describes an end-time feast: "Blessed are those who are invited to the marriage supper of the Lamb" (19:9). The fulfillment of this began in the life of Jesus and the early church.

In one sense, then, eating together is a foretaste of heaven. Especially as the church gathers to enjoy food and fellowship, we anticipate the joyful celebration around the throne of God. Heaven is often portrayed as a place of feasting, and we need a theology of feasting as well as of fasting.

Will we actually eat and drink at a great banquet in the new heaven and new earth? It seems so. At the last supper, after giving the cup to his disciples, Jesus said, "I will not drink again of the fruit of the vine until that day when I drink it new in the kingdom of God" (Mark 14:25). God has given us good things like food and drink to point to the great feast that we will enjoy with our Lord when he comes again in power and glory.

With this in mind, we should enjoy the things that God has given us in this life. Everything he has created "is good" (1 Tim. 4:4). God "richly provides us with everything to enjoy" (1 Tim. 6:17). It is not sinful to delight in what God has given us, as long as we eat and drink to the glory of God (1 Cor. 10:31). How do we do that?

First, we remember that the enjoyment of good things like food and drink points to our enjoyment of God himself. The pure joy of eating and drinking a good meal should remind us of the greater joy of pursuing God in his glory. Even the best meal will not satisfy us. We will be hungry and thirsty again. More importantly, we are to drink deeply from the river of God's delights. We are to feed on the Lamb of God by faith. We are to feast on God as we seek his glory, primarily found in the revelation of himself in his Word. We are to taste and see that he is good as we worship and have fellowship with him.

The things of this world are vanity. They cannot compare to the true joy that is found in God. But they help point us to the greater delight of God himself.

This leads us to the second way that we eat and drink to the glory of God, namely, by enjoying God *in* the things that he has given to us. Our enjoyment of the good things of this world is not true enjoyment if we delight ourselves in the gift and not in the Giver.

In his sermon "Satisfaction in God" Cotton Mather states,

Our continual *apprehension* of God, may produce our continual *satisfaction* in God, under all His dispensations. Whatever enjoyments are by God conferred upon us, where lies the relish, where the sweetness of them? Truly, we may come to relish our enjoyments, only so far as we have something of God in them. It was required in Psal. xxxvii. 4, "Delight thyself in the Lord." Yea, and what if we should have no delight but the Lord? Let us ponder with ourselves over our enjoyments:

"In these enjoyments I see God, and by these enjoyments, I serve God!"

And now, let all our delight in, and all our value and fondness for our enjoyments, be *only*, or *mainly*, upon such a divine score as this. As far as any of our enjoyments lead us unto God, so far let us relish it, affect it, embrace it, and rejoyce in it: "O taste, and feed upon God in all;" and ask for nothing, no, not for life itself, any further than as it may help us, in our *seeing* and our *serving* of our God.[2]

This should caution us against an unbridled pursuit of the things of this world. Paul reminds us of the danger of this kind of pursuit (1 Tim. 6:9–10). While God gives us good things to enjoy, we must pursue the Giver, not the gift. We need to remember that a godly self-denial is essential to the Christian life. Jesus said, "If anyone would come after me, let him deny himself and take up his cross daily and follow me" (Luke 9:23).

As Jesus is a model for enjoying the good gifts of God, so Jesus is our model of self-denial. He did not think equality with God something to be held onto for his own advantage but made himself of no reputation. He became a man to be despised and rejected, giving up for a time the honor of being recognized and worshipped as God. He had no place to lay his head. He was mistreated, suffered, and gave himself over to death. So the Christian must deny himself and take up his cross.

Jesus was the most contented man who ever lived. In the same way, Burroughs writes, "there was never any man or woman so contented as a self-denying" one. He goes on to say, "A discontented heart is troubled because he has no more comfort, but a self-denying man rather wonders that he has as much as he has."[3]

But self-denial does not equal grim austerity. We deny ourselves because we are followers of Jesus, and we seek first his Kingdom and his righteousness. We do not pursue the things of this world. Yet our lives are to be marked by joy, and we can delight in the things of this world as we recognize them as gifts from God. We delight in God in them. They point us to the greater delight of God himself. Joy and satisfaction come only in the restless pursuit of the pleasures of God.

At the end of the day, this is the essence of Christian contentment. Enjoying (finding joy in) God. Delighting and resting in him.

At the same time, this is the essence of godliness. Godliness ultimately consists in beholding, by faith, the glory of God revealed in Jesus Christ and in delighting and resting in that glory. The heart of godliness is seeing God and savoring him. Nothing in the world compares to this.

Godliness with contentment is great gain. Only one thing is necessary.

Discussion Questions

1. In your own words, summarize the meaning of Paul's phrase "godliness with contentment." What are the practical implications of the fact that godliness and contentment are so closely tied together? Is it correct to say that pursuing godliness means pursuing contentment and that pursuing contentment means pursuing godliness? Why or why not?

2. How does the biblical truth that we are pilgrims and strangers in this world help us in our pursuit of contentment?

3. Scripture says that God has created all things for our enjoyment (1 Tim. 6:17). Yet we are also called to recognize the vanity of the things of the world and to live a life of self-denial. How can we reconcile these things?

4. How can our enjoyment of the good gifts of this life help us in our pursuit of contentment?

5. Think of practical ways in which you can develop a lifestyle of seeing and savoring God.

Notes

Preface

1. Jeremiah Burroughs, *The Rare Jewel of Christian Contentment* (1648; repr., Carlisle, PA: Banner of Truth Trust, 2000).

2. Thomas Watson, *The Art of Divine Contentment* (1653; repr., Glasgow: Free Presbyterian Publications, 2001).

Introduction

1. J. C. Ryle, *Thoughts for Young Men* (1887; repr., Amityville, NY: Calvary Press, 1996), 23.

2. New York: Random House, 2003.

3. John Piper, "We Want You to Be a Christian Hedonist!", *Desiring God*, August 31, 2006, http://www.desiringgod.org/resource-library/resources/we-want-you-to-be-a-christian-hedonist.

Chapter One: The Nature of Christian Contentment

1. Burroughs, *The Rare Jewel of Christian Contentment*, 21.

2. See John Ferguson, "The Triumph of Autarcy," in *Moral Values in the Ancient World* (London: Methuen and Co., 1958), 133–58. See also John Ferguson, *The Religions of the Roman Empire* (Ithaca, NY: Cornell University Press, 1970), 190–210. On the prominent theme of individualism in the ancient world, see Luther Martin, *Hellenistic Religions: An Introduction* (Oxford: Oxford University Press, 1987).

3. Burroughs, *The Rare Jewel of Christian Contentment*, 19.

Chapter Two: The Necessity of Christian Contentment

1. Leo Tolstoy, *How Much Land Does a Man Need? and Other Stories* (London: Penguin Books, 1993).

2. Burroughs, *The Rare Jewel of Christian Contentment*, 19.

3. Ibid., 127.

4. Ibid., 120.

Chapter Three: The Dangers of a Murmuring, Discontented Spirit

1. Richard Cecil, *Memoirs of the Rev. John Newton*, in *The Works of John Newton*, vol. 1 (Edinburgh: The Banner of Truth Trust, 1985), 108.

Chapter Four: The Contentment of the Discontented Christian

1. Burroughs, *The Rare Jewel of Christian Contentment*, 43.

2. Thomas Kelly, "Praise the Savior, Ye Who Know Him," 1806.

3. Samuel Zwemer, *Raymond Lull: First Missionary to the Moslems* (New York: Fleming H. Revell, 1902), 132–45.

Chapter Five: Finding Contentment in the Midst of Affliction

1. Tertullian, *Apologeticus*, 30.

2. Richard Stauffer, *The Humanness of John Calvin: The Reformer as a Husband, Father, Pastor and Friend* (Vestavia Hills, AL: Solid Ground Christian Books, 2008), 42.

3. Quoted in Dale Ralph Davis, *The Wisdom and the Folly: An Exposition of the Book of First Kings* (Ross-Shire, Scotland: Christian Focus, 2002), 90.

4. Quoted in Edward M. Bounds, *The Essentials of Prayer* (New Kensington, PA: Whitaker House Publishers, 1994), 7.

5. Roland Bainton, *Here I Stand* (Nashville: Abingdon Press, 1978), 237.

6. H. C. G. Moule, *Charles Simeon* (London: Methuen and Co., 1892), 266.

7. Samuel Rodigast, "Whate'er My God Ordains Is Right," 1675, trans. Catherine Winkworth, 1863.

Chapter Six: The Mathematics of Contentment

1. My understanding of Romans 7 is the classic Reformed interpretation. It is common, however, among interpreters today to treat Romans 7 as a reference not to Paul's (and therefore the believer's) struggle with sin, but rather to see Romans 7 as the struggle of the unbeliever. But this is clearly not the most natural reading of the passage. Paul's use of "I" and the present tense point to a present struggle in Paul's own life. He also clearly speaks from the perspective of one who is a new creation in Christ. He "delights in the law of God, in [his] inner being" (v. 22). Only a converted person can truly say that. Paul also says that he does not "understand" when he does the very thing he hates (v. 15). Why does he not understand it? Because at the core of his being, he is a new creation. Overall the traditional interpretation is superior.

2. Quoted in John Piper, *Let the Nations Be Glad!: The Supremacy of God in Missions* (Grand Rapids: Baker Books, 1993), 73.

Chapter Seven: The Contentment of Longing for Heaven

1. D. A. Carson, *A Call to Spiritual Reformation* (Grand Rapids: Baker Books, 1992), 61–62.

2. Jeremiah Burroughs, *A Treatise on Earthly-Mindedness* (1649; repr., Soli Deo Gloria, 2008).

3. Burroughs, *The Rare Jewel of Christian Contentment*, 75.

4. Anne R. Cousin, "The Resurrection and the Life Everlasting," 1857.

5. Don Cormack, *Killing Fields, Living Fields* (Tain, Scotland: Christian Focus Publications, 2001), 229–30. Copyright protected by OMF International, www.omf.org.uk/.

Chapter Eight: Finding Contentment in the Enjoyment of God

1. Augustine, *The Confessions of St. Augustine*, trans. Rex Warner (New York: Penguin Books, 1963), 17.

2. O. Palmer Robertson, *The Christ of the Covenants* (Phillipsburg, NJ: P&R Publishing, 1980), 15.

3. Moule, *Charles Simeon*, 266.

Chapter Nine: The Contentment of Being Conformed to the Image of Christ

1. Charles Spurgeon, *Morning by Morning: A New Edition of the Classic Devotional Based on the Holy Bible, English Standard Version*, ed. Alistair Begg (Peabody, MA: Hendrickson Publishing, 1991), 149.

2. See Ken Sande, *The Peacemaker: A Biblical Guide to Resolving Personal Conflict*, 2nd ed. (Grand Rapids: Baker Books, 1997), 36–40.

3. Francis Schaeffer, "No Little People, No Little Places," *No Little People* (1974; repr., Wheaton: Crossway, 2003), 21–32.

4. Ibid., 25.

5. Ibid., 26.

6. Ibid., 29–30.

Conclusion: The Riches of Godliness with Contentment

1. Blaise Pascal, *Pensees*, 1660.

2. Cotton Mather, "Satisfaction in God," *Fire and Ice: Puritan Reformed Writings*, http://www.puritansermons.com/reformed/mather1.htm.

3. Burroughs, *The Rare Jewel of Christian Contentment*, 89–90.

TRUTHFORLIFE®

Truth For Life is the Bible-teaching ministry of Alistair Begg. Our mission is to teach the Bible with clarity and relevance so that unbelievers will be converted, believers will be established, and local churches will be strengthened.

Since 1995, Truth For Life has accomplished its mission on the radio, online, and in print. Every day we release a new Bible-teaching message on over 1,500 radio outlets around the world and through our website and daily podcast.

A large content archive is available on our website, where listeners can download free messages or purchase CDs and DVDs of Alistair Begg's sermons at cost. Printed publications, authored by Alistair Begg, address a variety of life's challenges, yet always point back to the authority and truth of God's Word.

Truth For Life also connects with listeners at live ministry events and conferences across the U.S. and Canada in cities where the radio program is heard.

CONTACT TRUTH FOR LIFE

In the U.S.:
P.O. Box 398000, Cleveland, OH 44139
www.truthforlife.org • letters@truthforlife.org
1-888-588-7884

In Canada:
P.O. Box 132, Maple Ridge, BC V2X 7E9
www.truthforlife.ca • letters@truthforlife.ca
1-877-518-7884

And also at:
www.facebook.com/truthforlife
www.twitter.com/truthforlife